ASIA FUTURE SHOCK

Also by Michael Backman:

The Asian Insider: Unconventional Wisdom for Asian Business
Big in Asia: 30 Strategies for Business Success (with Charlotte Butler)
Big in Asia: 25 Strategies for Business Success (with Charlotte Butler)
Inside Knowledge: Streetwise in Asia
Asian Eclipse: Exposing the Dark Side of Business in Asia

Michael Backman

Asia
FUTURE
SHOCK

Business Crisis and Opportunity in the Coming Years

palgrave
macmillan

First published 2008 by
PALGRAVE MACMILLAN
Houndmills, Basingstoke, Hampshire RG21 6XS and
175 Fifth Avenue, New York, N.Y. 10010
Companies and representatives throughout the world

PALGRAVE MACMILLAN is the global academic imprint of the Palgrave Macmillan division of St. Martin's Press, LLC and of Palgrave Macmillan Ltd. Macmillan® is a registered trademark in the United States, United Kingdom and other countries. Palgrave is a registered trademark in the European Union and other countries.

ISBN-13: 978–0–230–00677–5
ISBN 10: 0–230–00677–9

This book is printed on paper suitable for recycling and made from fully managed and sustained forest sources. Logging, pulping and manufacturing processes are expected to conform to the environmental regulations of the country of origin.

A catalogue record for this book is available from the British Library.

A catalog record for this book is available from the Library of Congress.

10 9 8 7 6 5 4 3 2 1
17 16 15 14 13 12 11 10 09 08

Printed in China

Contents

Contents

Introduction

Not long ago we needed to look for a school for our son Shimon who was then not yet five. An interview with the headmaster was part of the application process for one north London school. It turned out that he would interview us rather than the other way round. The headmaster told us that the school was "very strong on Latin" and those boys who showed an aptitude for it would be permitted to go on to study ancient Greek, evidently a reward for having done well at Latin, judging by the glint in the headmaster's eye.

I was appalled. "Latin!" I said. "Why do you teach Latin? How many people in the world today speak Latin?"

"Err, well none, but Latin is the root of *all* languages," said the headmaster.

"What, you mean Chinese, Vietnamese, and Indonesian?"

"Oh, not *those* languages," said the headmaster, "I mean all European languages."

"Oh, the dying languages of Europe, like French. Do you know how many people in the world today speak Chinese?"

The headmaster shook his head. "I couldn't say."

"More than a billion." The headmaster looked surprised. "Do you have any plans to teach Chinese?" I asked.

"None. I can't say that I've thought about it."

I thought to myself: "You make young boys learn languages that no one speaks anymore and then ignore some of the most important languages in the world today – you idiot!" But then for many in London, Asia is still the *Far* East, with particular emphasis on the word "far" as if the Internet and jet aircraft are still to be invented.

The world is changing. Obviously a bit too fast for certain north London headmasters. But for others, such as corporate planners, business strategists, and – although they might not know it – the odd five-year-old, what Asia will be like in the next 10, 20 and 30 years is of immense importance.

Asia will be very different then compared with now. When Shimon is in his twenties, China will have the world's largest economy on a purchasing power parity (PPP) basis. The Economist Intelligence Unit (EIU) has estimated that by 2020, Asia will account for 43% of the world economy, up from 35% in 2005.[1] It won't be more important or richer than the West, but what it will be is more important than it is now – a rebalancing is underway rather than a revolution.

There will be 400 million more people in Asia than now. India will be close to being the world's most populous country and Mumbai will be the world's most populous city. Vietnam will have an economy like Guangdong's. North and South Korea probably will be reunited. Asia will be home to half the world's nuclear reactors. The world's biggest nation of English speakers will be China. Mandarin usage will swell by at least 50% in China too. And China will have a powerful navy and be a major exporter of sophisticated arms. A hundred million Chinese tourists will pour out of China every year. Large, sprawling Indian multinationals will range across the world's economies more than they do now. Important Asian companies will be controlled by charitable trusts. Africa will be wracked with ethnic tension but this time between Africans and Chinese migrants rather than Indians. There will be 20 million fewer Japanese than today. India and China will have as many as 250 million more men than women, possibly leading both to expand their armies after years of contracting them. And Indonesia and Malaysia will have run out of oil – both will rue the wasted opportunities of the preceding decades.

Asia's governments will increasingly allow their citizens more freedom, but not political freedom. Those countries that are not democratic now will have gone no closer to becoming democracies. And those that are democratic will have stepped away from it, to become more authoritarian. The model of economic and social freedom but without commensurate political freedom will be the model of choice as other alternatives have been tried and found wanting. Ruling parties in China, Vietnam, Malaysia, and Singapore increasingly don't much care what the citizenry do as long as they don't threaten their power. The emerging contract between Asia's governments and their citizenry is "let us stay in power and in return we will leave you alone and deliver economic growth and jobs." Media freedom is stifled and, ironically, the Internet is in the process of being press-ganged into serving Asia's autocrats rather than undermining them.

Myanmar's rulers would like to follow this model too, it's just that they understand almost nothing about economics. And those countries that do change governments – the Philippines, Thailand, India, and now Indonesia – have tended to underperform compared with the rest and will learn that fighting over wealth distribution before that wealth is created is a luxury they can ill afford. After all, democracy is the reward for building a good economy, not an ingredient for achieving one. No Western economy was ever a fully fledged democracy before it became seriously rich. Asia will learn this too.

Will the rule of law be strengthened in Asia? It will, but not evenly or quickly. It remains weak in most of Asia. That ought to be an unmitigated bad. But it isn't. Asia has actually found ways to profit from this. Consider healthcare. The cost of medical malpractice insurance is exorbitant in the US and directly contributes to the high cost of surgery in the US. Surgeons and hospitals in Thailand don't need such cover because the Thai legal system is poor and unpredictable and few patients bother to sue their doctors in Thai courts. Even if they did, any awards are unlikely to be substantial. And so Bangkok's hospitals are able to offer very competitive, high-quality surgery to foreigners who are willing to take the risk. Thousands of Americans and other Westerners are beginning to fly to Thailand for medical treatment. The trickle will become a flood.

Authoritarianism is going to pay dividends as well. Laboratory testing on animals is under threat in the West from animal rights activists. The irony is that they are not succeeding in having animal testing ended but shifted. They are helping to push it offshore, away from the gaze of Western regulators and an inquisitive media, to destinations like Singapore and Beijing where political activists have no voice and scientists can get on with their work unhindered. Stem cell research too is proceeding apace in Singapore because Singapore is not a plural society; interest groups are not given a voice and so little opposition can take root. It's the same with infrastructure development. China spends seven times what India does on infrastructure. Why? Partly because it can. The authorities in China do not face protests and court action each time they announce plans to build a new highway or power plant as is often the case in India.

Several years ago, a writer called Jim Rohwer wrote a book called *Asia Rising*. Asia promptly collapsed. "It doesn't do much for your credibility writing a book with a title like that," said Rohwer to me on the margins of a conference in Jakarta shortly after many of the region's currencies had plummeted and their economies were heading into recession. But the long-term trend is that Asia is rising. It's just that the route is not linear and Asia's economies are not rising at the same rate. It's the detail that matters.

As for Shimon, finally he was enrolled in a school in London that purposely encourages enrolments from children not born in the UK so that they can mix from a young age and learn about each other's cultures. So among his school friends today is a boy from Japan, one from China and a Muslim girl from Qatar. I hope he will be more global than me.

What follows are 25 important insights about Asia's future. They provide an introduction to some of the risks and opportunities in the coming few decades, a useful tool for business strategists and scenario planners. They might also be a tool for small boys and girls, or at least their parents, when it comes to deaming about their future careers. To the array of conventional choices like "train driver" or "nurse" might be added new fare such as "expert in Chinese corporate law with a proficiency in Mandarin" or "Indian corporate governance specialist."

Note

1   Economist Intelligence Unit, *Foresight 2020: Economic, Industry and Corporate Trends*, 2006.

Population Dynamics: How Asia's Face is Changing

▷ China and India's population will each reach 1.5 billion in the 2030s and, based on current trends, at some point India's population will overtake China's.

▷ But the current population of pre-partition India already exceeds China's by more than 100 million.

▷ 1.1 billion more people will live in Asia's cities in 2027 than in 2007.

▷ South Korea has the world's fastest ageing population. By 2050, more South Koreans will be aged over 50 than under.

▷ Current trends suggest that, by 2050, for every 10 people who work in China, there will be 7 not working – a massive dependency ratio of 70%.

▷ Singaporeans are dying out. For every 8 that die, only 5 are born.

The EIU estimates that, in 2020, China will be the world's largest economy on a PPP basis, with a GDP of US$29,590 billion, while the US will be in second position at US$28,830 billion. But China will be a long way short on a market-based exchange rate basis – US$10,130 billion compared with the US at US$28,830 billion. India will be the world's third biggest economy on a PPP basis, with a GDP of US$13,363 billion, and fourth biggest on a market-based exchange rate basis at US$3,228 billion.[1] Figures as large as these are mind-boggling, almost to the point of being meaningless.

Economists often talk about "economic fundamentals." But what is the ultimate fundamental? Surely it is people. After all, an economy is no more than people trading with one another. And so, over the long term, the fortunes of an economy are highly dependent on changes in population. What will happen in Asia in the coming decades? The first clue is to see how Asia's populations will change. Overall, Asia will have around 400 million people more in 20 years than at present. That's equivalent to the region adding on a United States and Japan. But Asia is not growing uniformly. The relative importance of Asia's countries in terms of population is going to change a lot.

India's population was estimated to overtake China's in 2030 when both countries were expected to have populations of around 1.4 billion. But in early 2007, China's State Population and Family Planning Commission released new figures suggesting that China's rate of population growth is slowing but not as fast as expected and that, by 3033, China's population will be 1.5 billion.[2]

Meanwhile, the population of the developed world is now virtually stable and unlikely to grow.[3] But already South Asia is the clear winner in the population stakes. Had partition not taken place in 1947, then India would have overtaken China for the number one spot years ago. The combined population of pre-partition India today (India, Pakistan, and Bangladesh) is 1.445 billion, compared with China's population of 1.322 billion. So already, South India represents a larger consumer market in terms of sheer numbers than does China. But spending power in China is far greater and the difference is growing.

Today China represents 39% of Asia's population and South Asia 40%. But China's relative importance will decline further, not just compared with India and the rest of South Asia but compared with all of Asia. It has one of the lowest population growth rates in the region, due to the success of its one-child policy and also its rising wealth levels – richer people tend to have fewer children. South Asia, on the other hand, continues to have one of the region's highest rates of population growth. Indeed, the population of pre-partition India is expected to expand in the first half of this century by 900 million people.

Not only will China's population be overtaken by India's in 2030 but it will then start to fall. Taiwan, Japan, South Korea, and Singapore will also experience declining populations in the coming decades. Japan's population will probably have peaked around 2007 or 2008 (the peak won't be clear until some time after the event). South Korea's population will start to fall in 2027, and Taiwan's in 2029.[4] Singapore's is more difficult to predict because its government is likely to permit even higher levels of immigration to try to avert a decline. But as things stand, Singapore's residents might be increasing in number but the actual number of Singaporeans will start to fall.

Each of these countries faces quite different challenges to Asia's other countries. Ways must be found to raise productivity to compensate for the shrinking pool of workers or else total GDP will fall. And the health and income needs for an expanding number of retirees must be catered for.

Elsewhere in Asia, countries that maintain high birth-rates – such as Bangladesh and the Philippines – face other challenges. How will they find jobs for all the new entrants to the labor force? How can they guarantee sufficient food? And how can they manage their environments in a sustainable way in the face of increasing and not just static population pressures?

Although Asia's population overall is rising, it is rising more slowly than before. Population growth is slowing due to a combination of factors, the most fundamental of which is wealth. In the parlance of economics, children are an "inferior good": as income rises, the demand for children also rises but by proportionately less. Contraceptives probably have little to do with it. People know how not to get pregnant even if conventional contraceptives are unavailable. It's simply that as people grow richer, they don't need to have so many children to support them in their old age, and their consumer preferences change. They want to spend their money and their leisure time on other things.

Greater income allows people access to new opportunities that make raising children more difficult – they want to eat out more, travel, pursue hobbies. Also, as countries become wealthier, female participation in the labor force rises. Women put off having children and they have fewer children while they pursue their careers. Increased workforce participation by women also means that many will decide that they don't need a husband to provide income security – they can do it for themselves. One final factor why people have fewer children as economies mature relates to domestic help: maids and nannies become more difficult and expensive to hire and extended families become smaller so that there are fewer relatives to help with child rearing.

Exploding Urbanization

Asia is urbanizing. People everywhere are leaving farming and heading to the cities. In China, the rush to China's coastal cities that is currently underway is the biggest migration of humans in the history of mankind. The process is speeding up. In the next 20 years, another 1.1 billion people will live in Asia's cities than do already.[5] Table 1.1 shows what is happening. Many of Asia's cities are growing naturally even without migration. But with natural population growth and migration, urbanization is exploding. Cities in the Philippines, Indonesia, Malaysia, Thailand, and Vietnam will almost double in size in the next 20 years. Can Asia's cities cope? No, is the short answer. Few can cope with their existing populations.

Table 1.1 Population and urbanization growth for selected Asian countries

Economy	Total population (million)		Urban population (million)	
	2000	2020	2000	2020
Indonesia	224.1	287.9	91.9	168.2
Japan	126.9	124.1	99.9	102.5
South Korea	47.3	51.5	38.7	46.0
Malaysia	23.3	34.4	13.4	23.6
Philippines	79.7	111.3	46.7	79.5
Thailand	62.4	71.9	12.4	19.2
Vietnam	78.5	99.9	18.9	34.7

Source: Coyle, W., Gilmour, B. and Armbruster, W. "Where will demographics take the Asia-Pacific food system?" in *Amber Waves*, USDA, 2003.

China's cities will have grown by at least 300 million by 2020. Correspondingly, the population of rural China is likely to be 145 million less.[6] Already around one hundred Chinese cities have populations of one million or more within their official boundaries. If suburban sprawl and satellite settlements are taken account of, then the figure rises to many more. Many big Chinese cities have barely been heard of outside China – cities like Changchun, Zibo, Changsha, and Handan – each of these has a population of well over a million.

Massive internal migration in China is churning and mixing the country's population. Many of the residents of Shanghai are no longer Shanghainese, for example. They come from across China and have their own regional dialects and accents, so that within the broad confines of "Chineseness," many of China's cities are newly cosmopolitan: Yunnanese mix with arrivals from Inner Mongolia, for example. The southern coastal province of Guangdong, which is about the size of Denmark, has attracted 30 million migrants in the past few decades. It was deemed to have 110 million residents in 2005, replacing Henan province in central China as China's most populous. It is now one of China's richest too, in terms of GDP per capita.

India too is urbanizing. Currently, Mumbai has a population of around 19 million. Soon it will have a population greater than all of Australia (currently 21 million). And by 2020, its population will be 28.5 million, by which time, it will be the world's most populous city, pushing the current leader, Tokyo, to second place. By then, four other South Asian cities, Dhaka, Calcutta, Delhi, and Karachi, will also be among the world's 10 most populous cities.[7]

And like China, India has many big cities that are barely known by the rest of the world. Indore, Ludhiana, Thana, Vadodara, Nashik, Meerut, Rajkot, and Aurangabad are among them – each has an official population of well over one million and actual populations that are much higher.

Rapid urbanization has many implications other than the obvious of where to house everyone and what to do with their effluent. Education is a big issue. Those who migrate tend to be younger and so of child-bearing age. Food is also a factor – not just quantity but the food mix. Urban diets are different from those of rural people. Animal products, fruit and vegetables are substituted for traditional rural food staples such as grains and tubers such as cassava. Work in urban areas tends to be more sedentary and less physical than in rural areas and so those in urban areas tend to have lower caloric needs. And diets become more diverse as people urbanize. Urban people also tend to eat out more.

Asia's growing urbanization also means that increasingly Asians are moving closer to the sea, as most of Asia's major cities to which internal migrants are drawn tend to be coastal. This also allows for a change of diet – for example more seafood. But coastal cities tend to have ports, which mean greater access to imported foods and other products. So growing urbanization is as much a factor for the fast-food, restaurant and catering industries, for example, as income levels.[8]

Other implications relate to healthcare, traffic congestion, crime control, jails, and even cemeteries. The disposal of the dead is a logistics nightmare for many Asian cities, particularly those with large Islamic populations for whom cremation is not an option. Jakarta is a classic case. Hectares of what has become prime Jakarta real estate now comprise cemeteries in this city where most people still source their drinking water from shallow ground wells. It's little wonder that intestinal and gastric disease is rife in Jakarta.

Ageing Asia

Better health and diet are leading people across Asia to live longer: average life expectancy rose by about 1% per year across all of Asia in the 1990s.[9] South Korea, China, Hong Kong, and Singapore now have life expectancy levels that match Western levels. And Japan's generally exceeds them.

The populations of Japan, China, Singapore, and Taiwan are all getting older but South Korea's is ageing fastest. In fact, it is believed to be ageing faster than anywhere. The share of South Korea's very elderly – those aged 80 or more – is expected to almost quadruple by around 2022.[10] And by 2050, the median age will be around 52 years. Reunification is one policy goal that South Korea can pursue to remedy this – North Korea has a much younger age population profile.

In any event, an ageing South Korea is manageable from the perspective of the South Korean government because South Korea, like Japan, is rich. But what about China? Thanks to its one-child policy, China is expected to reach Europe's current population age profile in 2030. There is a danger now that China will get old before it gets rich. It has a population age profile more like Malaysia's but an income level more like the Philippines and, in rural areas, income is more akin to Bangladesh.

China's elderly already number more than the entire populations of many industrial countries. By 2030, some 300 million Chinese will be classed as elderly. The UN's Population Division has forecast that, by 2050, the median age of China's populations will be around 45 years – more than the US at 41 years or the UK at around 42 years.[11] By this time, around a third of the Chinese population will comprise retirees. The ratio of workers to retired people will decline from around six to one now to about two to one.[12] The problem is partly due to retirement ages in China being relatively low – 50 for women and 55 for men – so this will be alleviated by raising China's retirement age to bring it more into line with international practice. Inevitably, China will have no choice but to do this. Indeed, ultimately, retirement ages in China will need to be among the world's highest rather than lowest.

Importantly, the pace of ageing in China is far greater in urban than in rural areas. Also, China has a growing lack of females compared with males (see Chapter 12) and this will mean that traditional caregivers – women and more particularly wives – will be in short supply to take care of China's elderly. Nursing homes, long an anathema in Asia which prefers that families take care of the elderly, might need to become commonplace in China to take care of all the elderly men that China will have in coming decades.

Assuming China's per capita income continues to grow strongly (and that is a big assumption), then GDP per capita could quadruple by 2022 and grow eightfold by 2030. But even with such a stellar growth performance, GDP per capita in 2030 will still only be 40% of the GDP per capita that prevails in the EU-6 countries today. (The EU-6 comprises France, Germany, Italy, Poland, Spain and the UK.) But by then, China will have Europe's current age profile. Two factors will soften this looming problem. GDP per capita will be higher on a PPP basis, and China's elderly of tomorrow do not have European-like income expectations for their retirement. Nonetheless, China's policymakers do face a big and unusual problem. Its growing pool of elderly will need to be supported, even if not at European levels of retirement income.

Another way of looking at China's plight is the dependency ratio – the number of people too old and too young to work divided by the working age population. One study has found that this ratio will start to rise by 2010. By 2030, this ratio will be around 50%, compared with less than 40% now. By 2050, it will be around 70% – meaning that for every 10 Chinese workers, there will be 7 not working.[13]

So how does China fund its pension system? The system is very much in a state of flux and awaiting resolution. No longer is there a single, unified scheme. This reflects the enormous change that China's economy has endured in the past two decades. The government has begun to replace the fragmented pension system in urban areas for which state enterprises had largely been responsible. In place is a mixture of mandatory contributions, mandatory defined benefits, and voluntary contributions.

This new scheme covers less than half the urban workforce and remains underfunded, partly because contributions are being used by local authorities to fund the benefits of current retirees, plus there have been some enormous corruption scandals involving pension funds. In 2006, the Chinese press agency Xinhua reported that US$2 billion had been embezzled from the country's public pension funds since 1998.[14] And in another development that year that did little to inspire confidence in the nation's pension schemes, a senior official at the National Council for Social Security Fund, which managed almost US$30 billion in pension funds at the time, was executed, apparently for spying for Taiwan.[15]

As for rural workers – their pension system has fallen apart altogether. Perhaps less than a quarter of China's workers are covered by the new scheme and so most workers either make provisions privately for their old age or make no provisions at all. In the past, the elderly were supported by their children but with the one-child policy, few younger Chinese today have siblings and that is going to put an intolerable burden on many.

China will need to face up to the problem of inadequate provisions having been made for retired rural workers in the coming decades. One option will be to determine property rights for rural households – assigning them the land which is essentially theirs but to which they don't have clear title. This would give them tradable wealth, so that they could sell the land, the proceeds of which could then provide them with retirement funds.[16]

Ageing populations lead to dramatic changes in consumption patterns. Household goods are acquired less. Less is spent on clothing. Expenditure on leisure travel rises. Older people eat more fresh fruit, fish, eggs, and vegetables.[17] And so countries with rapidly ageing populations should experience a marked decline in red meat consumption per capita, for example. Older people also are less likely to eat out. They might, at least for a time, eat out more in the evenings than ever, but they are more inclined to eat their midday meal at home. Younger people, of course, tend to be working and eat lunch away from the home even if it's in a staff canteen. This too has big implications for the structure of the food industry, particularly in places like Japan with all its fast-food bento box restaurants designed for office worker lunches. And when older people do eat out, their preference is not for fast food but full service restaurants. These are just a few considerations. But the biggest remains: who will support the elderly and by how much taxes will need to rise to cover the cost.

Falling Poverty

Economic growth has dramatically reduced absolute poverty across Asia. In just a generation, hundreds of millions have been lifted from absolute poverty. The International Labour Organization estimated that the percentage of people in South Asia living on US$1 or less per day had dropped from 40.9% in 1990 to 28.4% by 2004. In East Asia (including China), the figure fell from 31.2% to 14.9%.

However, hundreds of millions remain in poverty. The ILO also found that despite economic growth, the number of people in Asia living on US$1 or less a day was still around 600 million – or about two-thirds of the world's chronically poor. And if the measure is lifted to US$2 per day, then the number in Asia living on this or less blow out to 1.9 billion.[18] It's a reminder that with all the good news about record levels of economic growth in China and India and India's extraordinary successes with IT and outsourced back-office processing, the problem of poverty in Asia remains very real and very big.

Physical Changes

Better nutrition is changing the face of Asia, literally. Contemporary accounts written by Europeans who traveled to Southeast Asia in the eighteenth century make no mention that the locals were physically small. In fact, they described the locals as being about the same height as Europeans. It was only after about 1800 that a discrepancy began to appear – when European nutrition levels began to improve.[19]

The importance of nutrition on physical stature will be apparent even today to anyone who flies from Heathrow to any airport in Australia. As soon as they disembark, they will notice how suddenly the people are physically bigger (as opposed to fatter) than those they left behind. In China, Shanghai has long been the wealthiest part of China, and Shanghainese are known for being tall. And in Southeast Asia, it is remarkable how people's physical stature corresponds to the work they do and thus their incomes. Even within an office in, say, Jakarta, it will be noticeable that the local senior managers are physically far more impressive than, say, the office boy or the cleaners. This doesn't always hold, but on average, it seems to.

What this means is that as poverty reduces across Asia, Asians on average are getting physically bigger: they are getting taller and have bigger frames. This has implications for planners when it comes to designing public spaces, for example headroom in shopping malls, handrails on staircases need to be shifted up, and the meaning of eye level changes when it comes to displaying merchandise. Asian airlines are having to increase the space between seats, and the rows of seats in cinemas need to be further apart. Clothing and footwear retailers in Asia must now stock a wider range of sizes. Sports equipment manufacturers must change their designs. The shafts of golf clubs must be longer. And drug doses need to be changed.

Singapore's Demographic Time Bomb

Singapore is one Asian country that has become wealthy and must now deal with the issue of a shrinking population. It is handling the problem by increasing immigration. But that introduces a new complication: the locals feel that their city is being lost to new arrivals who take the better jobs and force up property prices. It is also changing the ethnic mix of Singapore, and its culture. It raises the question of what is a country like Singapore? Is it more than a location; more than a venue for a temporary population of expatriates?

Oddly, former Prime Minister Lee Kuan Yew said in late 2006 that Singapore's projected population will be 7 million by 2030. This appeared more aspirational than factual. Singapore's population has no chance of reaching anything like that unless immigration is radically lifted. The birth-rate needs to be 2.1 to replenish its population naturally (meaning that each woman in Singapore needs to give birth to 2.1 children on average just for the population to stay the same). But the birth-rate has now reached a historical low point – in 2005 for example, it was 1.24, the same as it had been the year before.[20] This implies an annual shortfall of 14,000 babies against the number needed simply to keep Singapore's population steady. Not only that, but fertility is falling fastest among the Chinese population, meaning that the overall proportion of ethnic Chinese is falling. In 1957, there were 6.48 babies per Chinese female. By 2005, the figure was 1.08.[21]

Singapore's government will not openly admit to it but it would rather keep the mix of Chinese versus other races at existing levels. And so it is more sympathetic to allowing settlement in Singapore of ethnic Chinese from other countries, particularly Indonesia and Malaysia. But if the population is to reach 7 million by 2030, then one in every two people residing in Singapore will not have been born there. What will be the implications of that for Singapore's cultural makeup? What will it mean to be Singaporean? What will it mean for the government? Will so many foreign-born residents put up with the paternalism and micromanagement that Singaporeans accept from their government?

Ageing populations mean shrinking workforces. A stopgap measure in Singapore has been for elderly Singaporeans to be attracted back to the workforce. The labor force participation rate for older Singaporeans reached a historic high in 2006. Almost 44% of those aged 60–64 were participating in the workforce compared with 32% in 1996.[22]

The government has tried a variety of schemes to encourage Singaporean woman to have children. In 2004, tax incentives and subsidies aimed at encouraging greater family formation were estimated to be worth the equivalent of 0.5% of Singapore's GDP.[23] Such measures appear to have largely failed. Why? Because Singaporeans are wealthy now. Poorer people tend to have more children and wealthier people do not. Singapore's lack of fertility is a function of its economic development. So migrants will need to be admitted, which means that, increasingly, the character of Singapore will change. Already, Indonesians, particularly those of Chinese descent, are very evident in Singapore. Malaysian Chinese are less visible but make up a huge proportion of Singapore's resident population. Chinese from mainland China are also more evident.

One option for Singapore is to attract back Singaporeans who have left Singapore. Between 2–5% of Singapore's population are believed to live overseas. But many have left because they are not comfortable with the government's controlling practices and its preference for micromanagement. They have left Singapore because they do not like Singapore.

But the main means by which Singapore will need to attract more residents is via the "foreign talent" program, whereby skilled expatriates are attracted to live and work in Singapore, many of whom might be granted citizenship. But again, while many educated and skilled foreigners might be superficially impressed by Singapore's relative cleanliness and efficiency, many do find the Singapore government overbearing. Whatever answer the government comes up with, one thing is certain: in 20–30 years the average Singaporean will be quite a different animal from now.

Suggestions for Business Strategists and Scenario Developers

► Population-wise, the relative importance of the various Asian economies will change considerably in the coming decades. These changes need to be incorporated into medium to longer term business strategies.

► Labor forces are changing too. Many will shrink, affecting wage competitiveness. China's, for example, will shrink considerably, whereas those of "younger" countries such as Vietnam and Thailand will not, meaning that changing demographics alone will see China's wage competitiveness decline in coming decades compared with other countries in the region.

► Asia's cities are growing quickly. Most major cities are coastal. This will reduce distribution costs – more and more people in Asia are relocating closer to ports.

► The rapid urbanization is creating massive logistics nightmares for urban planners in terms of water distribution, sewerage disposal and the like. Huge opportunities in urban sanitation and planning are emerging across Asia.

► Retirement income provision is a huge, emerging sector across Asia. Many Asian governments will require help with providing solutions to ensure adequate retirement incomes, suggesting a major role for pension fund managers.

► Ageing will also change the structure of demand for many products and services. This will vary between countries and within countries. China's urban population is ageing more quickly than is its rural population, for example.

► Growing wealth means better nutrition and so people in Asia are physically changing. They are getting taller and their bodies bigger. Clothing and footwear manufacturers need to supply a greater range of sizes than before, for example. This need is magnified by greater migration within Asia, leading to a greater diversity within populations.

▶ Migration means that Asia's populations are becoming increasingly diverse. This also will lead to a growing restructuring of consumer demand. Singapore, for example, will need to dramatically increase immigration simply to keep its population stable. This will see the mix of products demanded in Singapore change to reflect its changing ethnographic composition.

Notes

1 Economist Intelligence Unit, *Foresight 2020: Economic, Industry and Corporate Trends*, 2006.
2 *The Age*, "China's population growth nightmare," January 14, 2007.
3 United Nations, *World Population Prospects*, 2005.
4 Coyle, W., Gilmour, B. and Armbruster, W. "Where will demographics take the Asia-Pacific food system?" in *Amber Waves*, USDA, 2003.
5 Asian Development Bank, press release: "'Asian urbanization global priority,' ADB vice president tells Manila conference," February 5, 2007.
6 Op. cit. Coyle et al., 2003.
7 Population estimates by the Washington-based Population Institute and cited in BBC News, "Bombay faces population boom," December 30, 2000.
8 Op. cit. Coyle et al., 2003.
9 Op. cit. Asian Development Bank, 2002.
10 Heller, P., "Is Asia prepared for an aging population?," IMF Working Paper, WP/06/272, December, 2006.
11 *The Economist*, "Staying young," July 16, 2005.
12 *International Herald Tribune*, "China is aging toward potential pension crisis," March 21, 2007.
13 *Business Times*, "China's population woes," August 29, 2006. The survey cited was prepared by Goldman Sachs.
14 *The Economist*, "Looting the aged," September 9, 2006.
15 *International Herald Tribune*, "China executes high official as spy for Taiwan," August 9, 2006.
16 This option is suggested in Heller, P., "Is Asia prepared for an aging population?," IMF Working Paper, WP/06/272, December, 2006.
17 Op. cit. Coyle et al., 2003.
18 *Business Times*, "Poverty in Asia reduced by growth in China, India: ILO," August 30, 2006.
19 Reid, A., *Southeast Asia in the Age of Commerce 1450–1680*, vol. 1, The Lands below the Winds, Silkworm Books, 1988, p. 48.
20 AFP, "Singapore aims to attract migrants as birthrate at all time low," August 6, 2006.
21 Tan, E., "Singapore: The missing babies problem," *ASEAN Focus* newsletter, September, 2006.
22 *Business Times*, "Record number of older people in S'pore workforce," February 23, 2007.
23 *Business Times*, "Govt to spend $300m more a year to wake the stork," August 26, 2004.

2

The Internet, Big Business and Freedom

▷ A new pattern of growth is emerging in Asia: economic freedom with political control. The Internet was meant to undermine totalitarian regimes. But for Asia's more authoritarian governments it will become an increasingly useful tool in the coming decades as they search and destroy dissidents and would-be dissidents. All the while, the greater flow of information afforded by the Internet will allow Asia to reap huge economic benefits otherwise denied by an underresourced conventional media.

Freedom and liberty in Asia face a new threat in the decades to come. It is the Internet. The Internet was to sound the death knell for authoritarian regimes, undermining their attempts at control, particularly in terms of the flow of information. But ironically, technological advances have turned this around. The Internet is now being used by Asia's authoritarian regimes to eavesdrop, hunt down dissidents, and further control the flow of information. It is a disappointing outcome. And it is likely to intensify.

Consider this: every computer has a unique IP address and every posting or visit to a website can be traced to the originating computer. This means that getting households wired to the Internet will give governments the ultimate surveillance tool – a spying device in every household and office. Never before has such a surveillance system been possible. And the beauty of this system, unlike, say, conventional bugging, is that those who are spied upon actually install the spying equipment themselves – their computers.

Such a level of knowledge and control is the stuff of dreams for Asia's autocrats. That is why the Internet is not quite the danger to autocratic regimes that it might first appear. It is fast becoming their tool. It will be used to accumulate evidence against potential activists, charge and jail them, all before the wider public ever hears their names. In 2005, for example, Shi Tao, a Chinese journalist, was jailed for 10 years for leaking to foreign-based websites an internal Communist Party directive. How was he tracked down? Via his computer's IP address. Internet email provider Yahoo! helpfully linked Shi's otherwise anonymous email to his telephone for the police.

It is little wonder that Asia's more autocratic governments are not too disturbed by the spread of the Internet among their citizenry. Singapore, for example, is now one of the world's most wired countries – almost 99% of the population, or almost every home, school and business, has access to broadband Internet. The Singapore government's Infocomm Master Plan launched in June 2006 calls for 90% of households to have broadband access and 100% computer ownership for households with school-age children. Indeed, the Singapore government monitors its people so much that it no longer even needs to conduct a periodic census by knocking on people's doors. It simply crunches through existing databases. Singapore's government is actually quite proud of this.

Some Asian governments are developing their own homegrown expertise at controlling what their citizens can see on the Internet. Others are buying in the expertise. Burma's military junta, for example, is making use of a firewall developed by US software company Fortinet.[1] Fortinet's web-filtering products initially were aimed at companies so that employees would be unable to view inappropriate material via their work computers. Governments are extending the use of such products to whole countries so that the views of opposition parties and dissidents can be screened out. Interestingly, the introductory pages on Fortinet's website are available in a range of European and Asian languages. But the page on web filtering is available only in English, Thai, Korean, Japanese, and Chinese (traditional and simplified).[2]

China Leads the Way

Already China is second only to the US in having the world's greatest number of Internet users, with perhaps only 8% of its population online. Soon hundreds of millions of Chinese will be Internet users. The Chinese government is making sure that it is prepared. It has developed a highly restrictive firewall around the Internet. It's built into each level of the Internet's infrastructure in China, including Internet service providers and routers. Against all expectations, it successfully blocks countless sites.

Google has quickly established itself in China by overtly making itself a servant of the government's authoritarian desires. It agreed in 2005 to demands from the Chinese government that it provide only a stripped-down version of its fare, including self-censoring its search engine as a condition for entry into China's Internet market. Accordingly, thousands of items that can be viewed on Google outside China cannot be accessed via Google's China site. Google's Chinese staff work closely with the Chinese government to ensure that results on Google.cn do not include text, images, or links that the Chinese government deems subversive. Type in "Dalai Lama" on Google.cn and only one photograph of the current Dalai Lama meeting Chinese officials is available. Type it in outside China and many thousands pop up. Images of the 1989 Tiananmen Square protests and crackdown are not available at all on Google.cn.

The OpenNet Initiative (ONI), a collaborative partnership between Oxford, Cambridge, Toronto, and Harvard Universities, says of China that its Internet-filtering regime is the most sophisticated of its kind in the world:

> Compared to similar efforts in other states, China's filtering regime is pervasive, sophisticated, and effective. It comprises multiple levels of legal regulation and technical control. It involves numerous state agencies and thousands of public and private personnel. It censors content transmitted through multiple methods, including Web pages, Web logs, on-line discussion forums, university bulletin board systems, and email messages.[3]

Getting website masters to register is another tool. In 2005, it required that all China-based websites and blogs register with the government or be closed down.

Filtering takes place primarily at the backbone level of China's network, although individual Internet service providers also implement their own blocking. Cisco Systems of the US is among the technology companies to have sold the Chinese government thousands of routers that allow filtering, although some keyword searches are blocked by gateway filtering rather than by the search engines themselves. Major Chinese search engines filter content by keyword and remove certain search results from their lists. Similarly, major Chinese blog service providers either prevent posts with certain keywords or edit the posts to remove them. In addition, cybercafés are required by law to track Internet usage by customers and keep that information on file for 60 days. Says ONI: "China's Internet filtering appears to have grown more refined, sophisticated, and targeted."

A tool that is already precise will be honed even more. The government openly says that it intends to go further. One study estimated that, by 2006, China had almost 16 million individual bloggers.[4] Wang Xudong, deputy minister for the information industry, said in mid-2006 that his ministry's next target was to develop technologies to regulate blogs. As it is, the Chinese government can and already has pressured service providers to remove offending blogs. In late 2005, the Chinese government sent a request to Microsoft that it remove a blog by well-known Chinese blogger Zhao Jing in which he wrote about the government's removal of top editors at a Beijing newspaper. Microsoft complied. It deleted the website without notice.[5]

In mid-2007, the government-backed Internet Society of China, which comprises China's major Internet companies, issued a new draft code of conduct. The proposed code required bloggers to register with their real names and government identification cards.

In another move that will give the Chinese government even more control, it has developed its own system of Internet domains that are in Chinese. So instead of ".com," ".net," and ".org" suffixes in Roman letters, China's new system will require Chinese character suffixes. Up until China did this, Chinese users could type a web address in Chinese until the Internet domain was reached that had to be typed as ".com" or ".cn" for China, for example. Developing this system is not essential to China controlling the Internet within China – it already does that. But there is the possibility that later China could disconnect completely from the international ICANN system of Internet domains and route all internal Internet traffic through its own domain servers.[6] This need not be a permanent arrangement. It could be done temporarily, for example if China were to experience further Tiananmen-like unrest.

The government does not win each Internet battle. But the war has gone more in its favor than most analysts had predicted. The Internet and SMS are both used in China today to organize public protests. In central Xiamen in May 2007, for example, a massive protest of thousands took to the streets as people protested against the construction of what they believed to be a dangerous petrochemical plant. Messages to coordinate the protest had been spread widely by SMS and then photographs of the protest were soon posted on the Internet. What can the Chinese government do? Generally, its response is to increase the number of individuals employed to monitor the Internet for sites to block. So far, this approach has been surprisingly effective. As for the Xiamen city government, it responded by signaling that it would require bloggers and other Net users within the city to use their real names when posting material on the Internet. How effective this would be was unclear: presumably city residents could simply post messages without using their real names on websites registered in other cities.[7]

Inspired: Vietnam, Burma, Thailand, Singapore, and Malaysia

While the Western world has watched on in dismay at China's success at censoring the Internet, many of Asia's other governments have watched with admiration and have been inspired by China's efforts. Vietnam's government has developed a technically sophisticated filtering capacity that is able to block hundreds of political and religious websites. It has used its technology to focus on "anonymizer" sites that are designed to allow users to bypass government filtering systems to remotely access blocked content. At least 10 Vietnamese have been arrested for using the Internet to conduct what the Vietnamese government claims is subversive political activity.[8]

Vietnam claims that it controls access to Internet sites largely to block sexually obscene material, but ONI could not find evidence that it is blocking any pornographic sites. Instead, almost all the sites that it blocks relate to politically or religiously sensitive material that could undermine Vietnam's one-party system.[9] It was also found to block many more Vietnamese-language sites than English sites. Most relate to Vietnamese dissidents. ONI concludes that:

> While Vietnam has fewer resources to devote to on-line content control than states such as China, the country has nonetheless established an effective and increasingly sophisticated Internet filtering system.

Vietnam is also planning to implement a state-controlled Vietnamese-language second-level domain. The plan is similar to China's new Chinese-language top-level domains. So feasibly it too could take Vietnam out of the World Wide Web in future but still claim to give its citizens Internet access.

Thailand is also beginning to show an interest in blocking access to the Internet. In mid-2007, for example, it blocked access to YouTube's site because of postings on that site which it deemed were derogatory to its King. A single incident but it was a precedent. Asia's governments are experimenting and learning how to control the Internet all the time.

Malaysia has been mulling over the idea of requiring all local bloggers to register with the government in an effort to censor their postings. But attempts to limit blogs registered in Malaysia would fail as bloggers would simply migrate to sites outside Malaysia. "Do they even understand how blogs work?" asked Marina Mahathir, daughter of former Prime Minister Mahathir Mohamad, who herself writes a blog.[10] If they don't now, they soon will.

Singapore also has an interest in filtering the Internet. Currently, its Media Development Authority (MDA) claims to block 100 symbolic sites that relate to pornography, extremist religion, or illegal drug usage. All other sites that relate to these subject areas can be freely accessed in Singapore. But rather than 100 sites, ONI was able to find only 8 sites that were blocked among 1,632 sites that could reasonably be assumed to be targeted. It concludes that, presently, Singapore's use of filtering is minimal but that it uses other measures to censor the Internet, particularly as it relates to local political groups and the ruling People's Action Party, and local religious and ethnic matters. These include threats of extremely high fines or even criminal prosecution as a result of defamation lawsuits, and imprisonment without judicial approval under the Internal Security Act. Thus, Singapore's filtering regime for political, religious, and ethnic material is primarily low-tech, yet nonetheless potentially effective.[11] However, in Singapore, media outlets are expected to be "partners" with the government. The MDA said in 2007 that it was looking at ways to expand its jurisdiction from the traditional print media and broadcast sector to new media markets.[12]

And in Burma, in addition to the firewall acquired from Fortinet, newly installed technology now enables the junta to monitor emails, blogs, and chat rooms. Local access to major email providers such as Hotmail and Yahoo! is blocked.[13] It is ironic that Burma and Vietnam, which in general terms are two of the world's most technically backward countries, should have among the world's more sophisticated means by which to restrict the Internet.

Google and Baidu: Big Brother and Little Brother

What will government control of the Internet mean for Internet companies such as Google and Baidu? Google is a monster. Its 2006 net profit was US$3.1 billion from revenues of around US$10.6 billion. And by mid-2007, Google had a market capitalization of US$147 billion – putting it ahead of the then combined market capitalization of every company listed on the Stock Exchange of Thailand (at US$140 billion), the Jakarta Stock Exchange (US$134 billion), and the Philippine Stock Exchange (US$75 billion). That a 10-year-old company that produces no physical assets could have a greater market value than all the companies listed on the Jakarta stock market is astounding.

Quite simply, Google is *the* Internet success story. Part of its secret is that it doesn't actually have to handle anything physical and that keeps down costs, unlike Amazon.com which physically handles anything from books to kitchen appliances. It also means that it can operate anywhere – Amazon is restricted to those countries with widespread credit card usage and a sound postage system, which excludes much of Asia. Google is not just profitable but hugely so. How much so wasn't known until the company was floated in 2004. Up until then, the company's founders Larry Page and Sergey Brin were sitting on one very big secret: Google had already turned them into billionaires. That's why they were in no rush to list it. They didn't need the cash; nor did they want to disclose their business model to outsiders as would be necessitated by IPO-related filings.[14]

So why has Google been so successful? It has a clever search engine. That's important to attract users. The other clever part is its advertising. If you do a search on Google, advertising related to your search usually appears along with the results. Put in "China hotels," for example, and apart from the list of websites mentioning this topic, a series of sponsored links for hotels and travel companies related to China appear to the right of the screen. Click on these and Google earns money whether you make a reservation or not. In this way, Google makes direct use of the intentions of people who are looking for things. Its advertising thus has the character of well-targeted direct mail.

It means that advertisers on Google do not spend money advertising to people who are not interested in their products. (Yahoo!, on the other hand, has been more dependent on banner advertising, which is less targeted.)

Around 80% of China's Internet users use Baidu as their primary search engine. Like Google, it offers a search tool that's ahead of the rest. It allows for searches in Chinese using Chinese characters but also via phonetic or pinyin renderings of Chinese words. This is useful when users know how to say a word but not how to write it in Chinese.

When Baidu listed on the Nasdaq in 2005, its shares rocketed to almost US$154. The shares were down to US$129 by mid-2007 (after having dipped as low as US$50), giving it a market capitalization of US$4.4 billion. Its 2006 revenues were US$838 million with net profits of US$302 million. It has come a long way in only a short time. Revenues in 2004 were just US$13.4 million.

The search plus targeted advertisements has worked well for Google, and Baidu has imitated Google – except that, whereas Google makes it clear those links that are sponsored and those that are not, Baidu makes it less clear. Indeed, for some searches on Baidu, the first few pages of search results comprise nothing but sponsored links. That might annoy some users but it's good for shareholders, and Baidu is, after all, a business.

The Internet is not turning out to be the threat to authoritarianism that it was supposed to be. Instead it will become a tool. With new filtering and monitoring technology, the world's autocrats have an incentive to hasten the roll-out of the Internet. So rather than harm the prospects of Internet companies like Google and Baidu, Asia's authoritarian governments will only add to their profitability. The Internet will remain the epoch-changing tool that it already is in the West. But in much of Asia, it looks likely that it will be just another state-controlled media outlet. It is consistent with the new Asia – new economic freedoms but not political freedom.

Suggestions for Business Strategists and Scenario Developers

▶ Internet usage is spreading rapidly in most of Asia, even in those countries with more authoritarian regimes. Those that are more authoritarian are realizing that the Internet can be censored effectively and it can be used to track down sources of internal opposition. And so rather than standing in the way of rising Internet usage, many are realizing that they have an interest in promoting its spread.

▶ This means that the Internet will be an effective way in Asia for advertisers to reach various targeted audiences. But selling direct to consumers over the Internet will continue to be problematic where such selling relies on distribution via the postal network. Many postal services in Asia are very poor for parcels, with theft rates being relatively high.

Notes

1 Crispin, S., "A quantum leap in censorship," *Asia Times*, September 22, 2006.
2 See www.fortinet.com.
3 OpenNet Initiative, "Internet filtering in China in 2004–2005: A country study," 2005.
4 *International Herald Tribune*, "China vows broad new censorship measures," July 1–2, 2006.
5 *The Nation*, "Microsoft flayed for deleting blog of Chinese govt critic," January 11, 2006.
6 *International Herald Tribune*, "China sets up system for Internet domains," March 2, 2006.
7 *Financial Times*, "Chinese city to tighten grip over internet," July 9, 2007.
8 Op. cit. Crispin, 2006.
9 OpenNet Initiative, "Internet filtering in Vietnam in 2005–2006: A country study," 2006
10 *The Age*, "Malaysia mulls blogger registration," April 5, 2007.
11 OpenNet Initiative, "Internet filtering in Singapore in 2004–2005: A country study," 2005.
12 *Sydney Morning Herald*, "Singapore regulator extends its media jurisdiction," March 27, 2007.
13 Op. cit. Crispin, 2006.
14 Lanchester, J., "The global ID," *London Review of Books*, January 26, 2006.

China's Military Buildup

3

> ▷ China is massively increasing its military expenditure. But it still spends nothing like what the US spends.

> ▷ Its militaristic interests have shifted from being political to commercial – China wants to protect its shipping lanes and its investments abroad, from deploying 4,000 Chinese troops in Sudan to protect its oil investments there, to renovating the army headquarters for New Guinea's army.

> ▷ China either has or soon will have a blue-water navy, with an indigenously designed and built aircraft carrier, its own AWACS aircraft and its own indigenously designed and built fighter jets.

> ▷ US-led arms embargoes on China have encouraged it to build its own high-tech weapons industry. As a consequence, China will emerge in coming decades as an exporter of sophisticated military hardware. Chinese-made fighter jets are likely to be part of trade deals, for example.

A lot of nonsense is written about China's military buildup. Much of it emanates from the US. The US seems perpetually in need of a foe. It helps to unite an otherwise disparate country. It's a common tool that governments use. China is using it too now. The demise of communism would otherwise leave a vacuum if not for the rise of nationalism, which has become China's new gelling agent, the tool China's leaders can use to coalesce disparate regions and ethnic minorities into one political entity.

China announced a 17.8% increase in its military spending for 2007. That was after a 14.7% increase in 2006, a 12.6% increase in 2005, an 11.6% increase in 2004, a 9.6% increase in 2003 and a 17.6% increase in 2002. On the face of it, these increases seem enormous. But because of its rapid economic growth, China needs to spend massively on defense if it is to keep its defense budget at a constant proportion of GDP. These increases are in excess of GDP growth but not wildly so.

Even with these increases, China's declared spending on its military is relatively low compared with what the US spends. China says that it spent US$30 billion in 2005. But the US spent US$400 billion and Japan spent around US$47 billion. Currently, China does not even have an aircraft carrier in service. The US, the UK, Russia, Italy, Brazil, and even Thailand are among the countries that do. In fact, China doesn't have a lot of things when it comes to military hardware. But it is getting them.

The CIA, however, asserts that a lot of China's defense spending is hidden and off-budget. It believes that China's military spending might be two or three times higher than acknowledged by China. This is undoubtedly true to a degree but then the CIA is not an impartial assessor of these things. It has to fight for resources too and overexaggerating the China threat bolsters its case. Further disquiet derives from the lack of transparency about how and by whom decisions are made in China's military establishment. President Hu Jintao is the nominal head of the military forces. He is also chairman of the Central Military Commission. But in practice it is not clear how much power Hu wields over the military.

At the same time as spending more on defense, China has been cutting the numbers of military personnel. It claims to have demobilized 200,000 personnel from 2003 to 2006. But after the cuts it still has the world's largest military, with 2.3 million active personnel. The cuts don't reflect a desire to be less militarized on the part of China. Rather they reflect China's greater use of sophisticated defense technology. Between 2001 and 2004, China is known to have spent US$10.4 billion abroad purchasing weapons systems.[1] Clearly China is moving from a defensive capability to an attack capability.

The US and the EU have arms embargoes in place on China. One US military contractor, ITT, agreed in 2007 to pay a US$100 million settlement for illegally allowing its night-vision technology to be transferred to China, for example.[2] And so China has sought to develop its own weapons industry. It buys much of its external purchases from Russia and Israel.

Where is all this heading? With more than a trillion dollars in foreign reserves, surging military expenditure, and diplomatic initiatives in Africa, South America, Central Asia, and the Middle East, China's rulers are beginning to exercise more power abroad rather than simply bolstering their positions at home. China's military capabilities are moving rapidly to beyond asserting its claims over Taiwan, which it regards as a renegade province. Weapons embargoes on China will not stop it from becoming a military power. They are only slowing the process. But what they are doing is ensuring that China will have a large and sophisticated weapons industry of its own. By 2030, not only will China be a military super-power, it will be a major manufacturer and exporter of sophisticated military technology, thanks to the embargoes.

Protecting Commercial Shipping Lanes

Throughout history, the foreign and military policies of the major powers have been determined by the need to protect commodities supplies. As Chicago-based economist David Hale argues, British foreign policy in the late nineteenth and early twentieth centuries was shaped by the desire for commodities security.[3] He points out that Britain nearly took the side of the Confederates during the American Civil War because of its large cotton imports from the American south. Britain went to war in South Africa against the Boers largely to control that country's gold deposits. And after oil replaced coal as the fuel for the Royal Navy, Britain greatly expanded its role in the Middle East. The US similarly went to war in the Gulf after Iraq invaded Kuwait in 1990 and then invaded Iraq itself in 2003 in part to reduce its reliance on Saudi Arabian oil.

China's booming economy means that it has a voracious appetite for raw materials. Much of these need to be imported. China has few oil reserves but by 2030 is likely to import as many as 7.3 million barrels of oil annually.[4] (This compares with projections for Japan at 6.8 million barrels.) China has huge copper needs but satisfies only 18% of these needs from domestic sources. Similarly, it satisfies only half its nickel requirements from domestic sources.

The importance of international trade to China's economic well-being raises the question of the extent to which it will develop a "blue-water" navy to protect the sea lanes of communication in international waters – to protect the merchant shipping that feeds China with the supplies that it needs of oil, gas, iron ore, and copper from countries as diverse as Saudi Arabia, Australia, and Brazil.

Most of China's trade goes through the Malacca Strait, the sliver of ocean between Indonesia's Sumatra and the Malaysian peninsular, and also the Bay of Bengal, both of which have more pirate activity than anywhere else. There were 118 incidences of recorded pirate attacks in the area in 2006 compared with 50 for the rest of the world, for example.[5]

China has plenty of incentive to develop a blue-water navy – a navy capable of keeping its shipping lanes open. It has made no open declarations of its intent in this regard. But there is no doubt that it is upgrading its capability.

It is upgrading its submarines. The Romeo and Ming-class conventionally powered submarines are being augmented or replaced by the more capable Song-class submarines, which are indigenously produced, and Kilo-class submarines, which China has acquired from Russia. Its small force of nuclear-powered submarines is being upgraded too. The old Han-class submarines are being replaced by the indigenously produced Type 093-class SSN.[6]

Three new classes of Chinese-made destroyers are being brought into commission – the Luyang I, the Luyang II and the Luhau – which will enable a single ship to provide antiaircraft defense not just for itself but for a formation of ships.

As mentioned, China doesn't have a single aircraft carrier. It is a question of when it will launch its first one rather than if. The Chinese government said in 2006 that it planned to design and build its own carrier. They are hugely expensive. Conventionally powered carriers can now cost around US$2.5 billion to build per vessel. Nuclear-powered carriers can cost almost twice that. Nor do they operate alone. They need supply vessels, associated aircraft, submarines, and advanced electronic surveillance for protection. The Chinese government did acquire one carrier from Ukraine, the Varyag, which is moored in the northern port of Dalian. Amusingly, China said that the carrier would serve as a tourist attraction but it seems more likely that it is being used for training. Possibly it might even be upgraded to become operational. The Australian government did sell China one of its decommissioned carriers in 1985 as scrap but it is believed that Chinese engineers carefully studied the vessel before it was dismantled.

Finally, China is emerging as the world's most important builder of merchant shipping. It should overtake South Korea by 2015 to become the world's biggest producer of all classes of ships, by which time it will have no less than 21 dry docks.[7] As it is, the shipping arms of South Korea's Daewoo and Samsung have set up shipbuilding facilities in China to save costs.

Protecting Chinese Commercial Interests Abroad

Protecting sea lanes is one thing but what about operations in other countries? The US has long sought foreign military bases in those countries that are important to it commercially. Might China also, for example, demand bases in Western Australia to protect its resource supplies there? The US has a base in the north of Western Australia. Shouldn't China have a matching base? Or in Africa? Or Central Asia where it has invested heavily?

China has already deployed 4,000 troops in Sudan to protect its investment in the oil pipeline which it co-developed with Petronas of Malaysia.[8] Sudan has been in perpetual internal conflict between its Christian south and Muslim north. Malaysia too has been involved in training Sudanese troops, presumably for much the same reason.

In another extraordinary example of China's dealings with the military of countries in which it invests, China paid for and renovated Murray Barracks, the headquarters for Papua New Guinea's defense force in 2004. And in 2007, it did the same for Government House, the official residence of Papua New Guinea's governor general (a position which functions as that country's head of state). The Chinese government has also paid for PNG soldiers to attend the National Defense University in Beijing, the Army Command College in Nanjing, and the Infantry College in Shijiazhuang, and it has provided the country's police force with vehicles. This is for a country in which China has mine and logging interests and where civil unrest and crime are notorious.

Increasingly too, Chinese nationals work for Chinese companies abroad. Dozens of mainland Chinese work temporarily in Australia to fill worker shortages there. In Afghanistan, the Chinese construction and engineering group China Railway Shisiju Group had around 100 Chinese nationals employed in 2004 building three World Bank-funded highways in projects valued at US$21 million.[9] Chinese companies were awarded roles in the reconstruction of Iraq too after Saddam Hussein's overthrow in 2003. Might China feel obliged to send troops abroad to protect its citizens in the more difficult foreign working environments? After all, the Constitution of the People's Republic of China states in Article 50 that: "The People's Republic of China protects the legitimate rights and interests of Chinese nationals residing abroad and protects the lawful rights and interests of returned overseas Chinese and of the family members of Chinese nationals residing abroad."

As more and more mainland Chinese live and work outside China, hostile action against them will become more common. Rebels in northern

Niger kidnapped a Chinese executive of China Nuclear International Uranium Corporation (Sino-U) in July 2007, claiming that Sino-U was helping Niger's government to fund arms purchases.[10] In the previous month, students at Islamabad's Red Mosque seized seven Chinese accusing them of operating brothels nearby. They were soon released. Several days before three Chinese were killed in Peshawar. All this prompted the Chinese government to ask the Pakistani government to increase its protection of Chinese citizens who reside in Pakistan.[11]

China is now a big investor in many developing countries: Nigeria, New Guinea, Gabon, Indonesia, Burma, and so on. Is the intervention in Sudan only the beginning of a new role for China's military in other countries? How will China respond if governments of countries in which it has investments or would like to invest call for military help to maintain control? Alternatively, will China actively work to topple regimes that act against its commercial interests in the way that the CIA is alleged to have done? The answer to all these questions is almost certainly yes. China will have the ability for such interventions and it has the incentives. The other thing that China will do is to supply weapons and military technology to countries that are under threat and are important suppliers of resources to China, in much the same way that the US and Britain arm Saudi Arabia to safeguard it as a supplier of oil. Will China trigger an arms race in Africa as it seeks to arm its commodity suppliers there? Quite possibly.

Reaching Out

China has started to play an active role on the world stage in international security issues. And an even greater role is assured. Prior to 1989, China shunned taking part in UN missions, believing that such missions represented interference in the domestic affairs of other countries. But then in 1989, it took part in the UN mission to Namibia. In 2000, it sent 15 peacekeepers to the UN's force in East Timor. In 2004, it contributed 550 troops to Liberia and then 175 to the Democratic Republic of Congo. And in 2006, it committed 1,000 troops to the UN force in Lebanon, making it one of the largest contingents in the UN mission.

More recently, it has become active at the UN in New York too. In 2006, it twice voted for Security Council resolutions – one condemning North Korea's missile launches in July of that year and another calling on Iran to cease enriching and reprocessing uranium. Historically, China was a passive Security Council member and typically abstained on anything sensitive. Chinese representatives have started to give press conferences and sound bites too, signaling quite a shift in China's approach to international security matters.

China is also becoming more interested in military involvement and cooperation in the region. It held joint military exercises in Kyrgyzstan in October 2002. Around 1,000 troops were involved from China, Russia, Kyrgyzstan, Tajikistan, and Kazakhstan. It was the first time that Chinese soldiers had participated in military exercises abroad.

And its navy has increasingly engaged in joint exercises with the navies of some European and Asian countries. In 2004, the Australian and Chinese navies engaged in a joint exercise for the first time, off the northeastern Chinese port of Qingdao. More joint exercises were held in 2005, this time in waters near Shanghai. Why the Australian navy? Australia has become a major supplier of natural gas and iron ore to China – to the point where China has become Australia's second largest trading partner. Both countries have an interest in keeping open sea lanes between them.

Greater Sophistication in the Air

A Chinese government report released in 2006 said that China intended to reduce the number of combat aircraft in favor of fighters:

> The air force aims at speeding up its transition from territorial air defense to both offensive and defensive capabilities in the areas of strike, air and missile defense, early warning and reconnaissance, and strategic projects.[12]

Again, this represents a seismic shift for China.

In 2006, China unveiled an entirely new, indigenous fighter jet, the J-10, an advanced, multirole aircraft designed by Chinese engineers with assistance from Russia and Israel. The jet is made by China Aviation Industry Corporation I, China's most important aircraft manufacturer. Up to 300 J-10s could be produced to supplement the Russian-designed Sukhoi Su-27 and Su-30Mk jets already in service with China's air force. The J-10 is one of the most advanced fighters in the world – the sort of aircraft that the US hoped to avoid with its embargoes. China now has something to offer other countries to sweeten trade deals – highly advanced fighter jets. Exports of this aircraft could see more than 1,000 produced.

China is also developing an indigenous early warning or airborne warning and control system (AWACS) aircraft. Such a system will allow China to project its power far beyond its borders and beyond what has been its main

military concern, Taiwan. The aircraft, known as the KJ-2000, is a conver-
sion of a Russian-made II–76 transport plane. For years China has attempted
to buy AWACS technology from Israel, France, Britain, or Russia. The US
strongly opposed this, forcing China to develop its own technology.

In January 2007, China successfully tested an antisatellite missile by
having the missile destroy a defunct weather satellite. This was after three
failed attempts to test a similar missile. China said that it had no intention
of sparking an arms race in space. The US had successfully carried out a
similar test in 1985.

India Responds

India and China have long been rivals. But India does not face the arms
embargoes that China does. For example, India has also been allowed to
acquire three AWACS aircraft – the very aircraft that China has desperately wanted but has been blocked by the US from acquiring.

India is building up its naval capabilities in part because of China's
buildup. It announced in 2006 that a new naval base would be established
on India's east coast, near Visakhapatnam. The base was expected to berth
two aircraft carriers, support ships, and submarines.[13] Part of the rationale
for the new base is to counter China's emerging naval power in the Bay of
Bengal and to exert control over India's sea lanes of communication,
which are becoming more important as it too becomes more important in
world trade. Like China, India is very dependent on the Malacca Strait –
around half of all its international goods trade passes through the Strait.

India is developing its own aircraft carrier that will be capable of operating a fleet of 30 aircraft including naval light combat aircraft and Sea
Harrier aircraft. India is also working on its own indigenous design
nuclear submarine.

India was the biggest purchaser of arms from Israel in 2006. It has
significantly ramped up its defense purchases in recent years. The Indian
government's 11th Plan allows for India to spend more than US$30 billion
on foreign-made weapons over 2007–12.[14] Included will be 126 multirole
fighters at a cost of more than US$6.5 billion.

Friend or Threat in Asia?

China has longstanding land and sea territory disputes with India, Japan,
and most Southeast Asian countries (in relation to the Spratley Islands), and

then of course there is the issue of Taiwan. Do other Asian countries see China as a military threat? China's increasing military sophistication is something that they need to take into account. But essentially, China is not expansionist. But there is a sense that rising nationalism in China could drive China's leaders to become more militarily aggressive than they otherwise would be. Still, the main concern for China now is resource security.

Slowly, China's military is becoming more engaged with those of other countries in the region, participating in joint exercises to build up trust. China's navy joined a multinational maritime exercise in early 2007 for the first time. It sent two missile-armed frigates to take part in antiterrorist maneuvers in the Indian Ocean, which included ships from Pakistan, the UK, France, Italy, Malaysia, and Bangladesh. China can be expected to increasingly take part in such exercises. Its interests are now aligned with those of most other nations: commerce not communism is what drives China now.

Suggestions for Business Strategists and Scenario Developers

► China's growing militarization need not be incorporated into future scenario development as a threat. China's interest in building up its military capacity is more to bolster its commercial interests than for geopolitical or ideological reasons.

► China is restructuring its armed forces away from manpower and in favor of greater technical sophistication. There are considerable opportunities for supplying equipment and peripherals to the PLA, subject to applicable embargoes.

► India is dramatically boosting its military hardware purchases largely as a response to China. There are fewer embargoes on defense sales to India and so correspondingly more opportunities.

Notes

1 *International Herald Tribune*, "Worldwide arms sales reached $37 billion in 2004, most in 4 years," August 30, 2005.
2 *International Herald Tribune*, "ITT may settle charges on China tech transfer," March 7, 2007.
3 Hale, D., "Will China need a blue water navy to protect commodity markets," background paper published by Hale Advisors LLC, Chicago, January 7, 2004.
4 Ibid.
5 *International Herald Tribune*, "Piracy at sea," February 2, 2007.

6 Cole, B., "China: The PLA Navy's developing strategy," *China Brief*, The Jamestown Foundation, October 25, 2006.

7 *International Herald Tribune*, "Managing China's rise at sea," August 4, 2005.

8 Op. cit. Hale, D., 2004.

9 *Financial Times*, "Chinese workers killed in attack on Afghan camp," June 11, 2004.

10 *Financial Times*, "Niger rebels hold Chinese executive," July 9, 2007.

11 Bloomberg.com, "Pakistan troops kill 50 militants in Red Mosque Raid," July 10, 2007.

12 As quoted in *International Herald Tribune*, "China builds a superpower fighter," February 6, 2007.

13 Ramachandran, S., "India navy drops another anchor," *Asia Times*, November, 2006.

14 Srivastava, S., "India's voracious appetite for arms," *Asia Times*, January, 2007.

4

20 Million Japanese to go Missing

▷ There will be at least 20 million fewer Japanese by 2030.

▷ More than 25 million Japanese are aged over 65 but only 18 million are aged under 15.

▷ Japan is the world's most racially concentrated country: 99.4% are ethnically Japanese.

Japan's population has just about peaked, meaning that shortly it will go into reverse, the first developed, modern nation for which this is the case. The peak will be around 127–8 million people. One estimate is that the population will fall by around 20% by 2030 to around 103 million, by 30% by 2050 and by 50% by 2100.[1] Japan's Institute of Population and Social Security Research forecasts that the population will fall to somewhere between 92 million and 108 million by 2050. The UN forecasts that it will decline to 105 million.[2] By 2050, 800,000 more Japanese will die each year than are born and the country will have more than a million people aged 100 years or more.[3]

The absolute number of Japanese women of childbearing age is in decline. In 1982, there were 30.4 million women aged between 15 and 49. By 2002, the number had declined to 28.8 million and by 2022 it will fall to 23.8 million.[4] The Japanese government discovered in 2004 that the fertility rates of Japanese women were falling even faster than had been believed, having dropped from 1.32 babies per woman in 2002 to 1.29 in 2004. It had only just enacted a new pension scheme that assumed a fertility rate of 1.39.[5]

Japan now has around 25.5 million people aged 65 or more – that's 20% of its 127.5 million-strong population. And the number of Japanese aged 65 or more is currently growing by about a million a year. And with just 18 million people aged under 15, there are now more people in Japan aged over 65 than under 15 – the only mature economy in the world where this is so. And one more statistic: in 1950, there were 12.06 Japanese of working age (15–64) per person aged 65 or older. By 2000, there were just 3.99. By 2050, there will be just 1.71. Japan, to put it mildly, has a problem.

Migrants? But We're Japanese

There should be no mystery as to why Japan's economy is perennially sluggish. Economies after all are nothing more than people trading with one another. And with both an ageing and shrinking population, an economy can hardly be expected to have sustained growth. So, what is the long-term solution? Certainly not another round of tax cuts, spending more on construction, or another loosening of monetary policy. After all, it doesn't matter how cheap the cost of borrowing money is, most 80-year-olds simply are not going to start up a new business.

The answer is to boost immigration. But by how much? UN demographers have calculated that just to stabilize Japan's population, it will need to have 17 million new immigrants by 2050. Those 17 million would represent 18% of Japan's then population. But how likely is that? Not likely at all.

Japanese society is one of the most homogeneous in the world. An astounding 99.4% of Japan's population are ethnic Japanese (the figure includes the indigenous Ainu people). The other 0.6% are almost entirely ethnic Koreans and some ethnic Chinese. Only the Koreans are accepted to any great degree and then only grudgingly.

The cultural tenets of modern Japan do not have a long history. Notions of national unity, the Darwinian struggle for national survival, and racial vigor and purity were borrowed in the late nineteenth century from Germany, which had only recently unified. It had forged a national identity based on *Kultur*. Political institutions were still brittle and so not yet a suitable focus for national expression. Instead, you belonged if your language was German and you were of German stock. To further forge a national identity, Germans were told that they were special, unique even. The Japanese were told the same.[6] Japan has never quite moved on. And so immigration is seen as almost subversive to the state and the national culture.

But immigration keeps labor costs low for menial jobs. It brings new ideas and methods into an economy. It helps to promote international trade because a lot of trade is done via ethnic and family networks. But most of all, it helps to rejuvenate an ageing population. Japan benefits from none of this. The US accepts around a million migrants a year. But that is the sum total that Japan has accepted in the past 25 years. Those that have been accepted have, by and large, been marginalized.

Japan can barely even bring itself to accept refugees. It is generous with foreign aid to help refugees as long as the refugees settle somewhere else. Of course, refugees themselves may not necessarily want to go to Japan. Leaving situations of intolerance and persecution to settle in Japan might be akin to jumping out of the frying pan and into the fire. The number seeking asylum in Japan each year is typically less than 300, compared with around 100,000 who seek asylum in the US or Britain. Japan did accept over 10,000 boat people from Vietnam and Cambodia in the late 1970s and 80s, a point it often makes in its defense. But then the US has taken more than a million Vietnamese since 1975, and Australia accepted around 140,000 Indochinese refugees, Canada the same, and France almost 100,000.[7]

Economic Future

Japan's economy has been through prolonged doldrums. Signs of growth soon lost their puff in the 1990s and early 2000s. And government efforts to foster them don't seem to work. Massive spending on infrastructure, government buy-ups on the stock market, and forcing interest rates to zero by flooding the economy with cash were all tried and essentially failed. Interest rates were kept low to encourage investment and consumer spending but instead many Japanese simply withdrew their money from banks and held it as cash because bank and building society fees and charges more than wipe out any interest earnings. At one point, market interest rates were actually negative.[8] By 2007, Japan's economy looked healthier. But the headline figures betrayed the hollowness of the growth: consumption data was flat. The growth was coming not from Japan itself but from exports. For growth to be sustainable, domestic demand needs to be the main driver of an economy. This is barely possible for Japan.

Demographics are at the heart of the problem. Japan simply doesn't have enough young people forming families and new households, with all the spending that goes with it, to keep the economy growing.

Instead, it has a lot of older people who are retired or are facing retirement, who have spent their lives acquiring all the goods they need and are now more concerned with looking after their savings. And those savings amount to a very large pool – the average savings balance of elderly Japanese households is a whopping ¥25.3 million, which is more than 50% higher than that for all households. Loosening these purse strings would go a long way to reviving economic growth. But how to do that? Should each retiree be required to have two hip replacements instead of one, or add on new bedrooms to their houses? Of course not. And when they do spend significantly, it's often outside Japan: tour groups of elderly Japanese have become a regular feature in Europe's capitals. The elderly cannot be a source of economic growth and no government stimulus package will ever make them that.

Not only is the higher spending base of Japan's population quickly shrinking as a proportion of the total but so too is the number of wage and salary-earning taxpayers. This is happening so fast that the next generation of Japanese will face a net increase in lifetime taxes of 170% on that faced by the current generation, assuming that the number of old people who will then be in Japan are to have the same government benefits that Japan's elderly currently enjoy.

Most of the rest of the world is used to the idea of buying property, particularly residential housing, with the reasonable expectation of making a capital gain. Speculating in residential property has become a profitable hobby for many Australians, Britons, and Americans. But in Japan, there's a better then even chance that a house or a flat bought today will be worth less in the future.

Can the Japanese property market pick up? Yes, but not in a sustained way. How can it when forecasters are projecting that in 50 years there will be 25 million fewer Japanese, or worse? Land prices for both commercial and residential areas fell for each of the years between 1991 and 2003, for example.[9] Prices for commercial land across Japan are now roughly equivalent to the levels they were in the late 1970s, before the asset bubble of the 1980s.

Growth can and does come from exports but Japan is not the export dynamo that it once was, thanks largely to the "hollowing out" of the Japanese economy in the 1980s, whereby a lot of Japanese manufacturing was shifted offshore to lower cost countries. In any event, the relative size of Japan's export sector was never as important to the Japanese economy as is commonly assumed. The American economist Richard Katz has pointed out, for example, that as a share of GDP, Japan's exports in recent years, at around 10%, are no higher than in the 1950s.

Japan's economy has become more open to outside investment. Foreigners have been allowed to take large and often controlling stakes even in Japanese icons like Mazda, Mitsubishi, and Nissan. This has certainly helped to revitalize companies that needed new management practices and new markets.

And so by 2007, the Japanese economy did seem to have revived. Growth returned after a very long slumber. Legislators, investors, and analysts were jubilant. But was the jubilance justified? Quite simply, the answer is no. Confidence in an economy tends to be self-fulfilling. But confidence is not an economic fundamental. No doubt the renewed vigor was also due to the seemingly impervious buoyancy of the world economy. After all, in a strong wind even turkeys can fly. Japan was being pulled along by the rest of the world. But the fundamental essence of the Japanese economy, its people, hadn't changed. Not only were they ageing faster than ever in 2007, but they were about to start disappearing.

Suggestions for Business Strategists and Scenario Developers

▶ The huge emphasis that past Liberal Democrat Party governments placed on construction means that many parts of Japan are now overbuilt. There are too many bridges, highways, conference facilities, exhibition centers, and the like. The price for the use of such facilities can only grow cheaper as Japan's population shrinks and its working age population shrinks even more. Japan increasingly will be a cost-effective international venue for conferences and conventions, for example. More movies will be made there. (The 2003 movie *Lost in Translation* is one example. Fifteen years earlier, the costs of filming in Japan would have made such a movie unthinkable.) And there will be an upswing in international tourism to Japan as on-ground costs become lower.

▶ Real estate as an investment might look superficially attractive as prices are now low compared with the boom times of the 1980s, but with a declining population, the long-term potential for capital gain is limited, especially when compared with other markets. The wisdom of foreign pension funds such as Singapore's GIC buying up big in Japanese property needs to be questioned.

▶ Industries that relate to the elderly will be one of the few strongly growing sectors in Japan. Healthcare, pets, dietary supplements, retirement homes, and leisure activities related to retirees and the elderly can all expect further growth.

▶ Sectors that relate to young people will contract. Japanese companies that produce products that appeal to the young will need to establish themselves overseas to expand. The youth clothing brand Bathing Ape is one example. It has established outlets in London, New York, and Los Angeles.

▶ Don't write Japan off as an export destination, particularly for high-end consumption goods. National income may not grow much more and it might even decline but GDP per capita is likely to rise. So in essence there will be fewer but richer Japanese.

Notes

1   Asian Demographics Ltd, "The year total population is projected to peak of each country in Asia," February 1, 2003.
2   *The Economist*, "The incredible shrinking country," November 13, 2004.
3   *International Herald Tribune*, "Outsiders waiting to be insiders," July 24, 2003.
4   Asian Demographics Ltd, "The changing age profile of mothers in Japan: 1982 to 2022," March 8, 2003.
5   *Financial Times*, "Japan waits for its angels to deliver," June 11, 2004.
6   See Buruma, I., *Inventing Japan: From Empire to Economic Miracle*, Orion Books, 2003, for more details on the creation of modern Japan.
7   *Far Eastern Economic Review*, "Don't come knocking," July 31, 2003.
8   *The Age*, "Rising sun benchmark below horizon," January 29, 2003.
9   *Bangkok Post*, "Japan's land prices continue to decline," March 25, 2003.

5

The Two Koreas to Reunify

▷ South Korea has the world's most rapidly ageing population. It needs reunification to give its ageing population a transfusion and to rejuvenate its labor force to restore competitiveness.

▷ North Korea needs it to head off an eternity of economic stagnation: GDP per capita in the South is US$24,200. In the North it's US$1,800.

One of the great tragedies of the 2003 invasion of Iraq and the subsequent debacle of its occupation is that it made an invasion of North Korea extremely unlikely. Iraq did not have weapons of mass destruction. But it is clear that North Korea does – chemical, biological, and nuclear. But more than that, overthrowing the government of Kim Jong Il would free 23 million North Koreans from being held hostage, which essentially is their current predicament.

US President George Bush famously damned North Korea as one of the "axes of evil" in a speech in January 2002, alongside Iraq and Iran. And for its part, North Korea delights in pulling stunts aimed at strengthening its hand in the international community, such as carrying out a nuclear test in 2006, albeit an unusually small one.

In any event, the North Korean regime will not last. Nor will North Korea. Reunification with South Korea is inevitable. The only question is when.

China remains North Korea's main backer. It maintains a "treaty of friendship" that it signed with North Korea in 1961, which commits China to defending North Korea if it is attacked. And although China was unhappy with North Korea's 2006 nuclear test, it does not countenance regime change in North Korea as an option. North Korea will have to implode of its own accord. It will do so the more that South Korea engages the North and North Koreans can see of what they have been deprived. South Korea needs reunification too. It faces two demographic crises: it has a serious gender imbalance particularly among younger South Koreans, but even more acutely, it is ageing faster than any other nation on earth.

The median age for South Korea's population is forecast to rise to 50.9 years by 2040, up from 36.8 now.[1] And by 2050 it will be around 52 years. This means that more than half the population will be aged more than 50 in a generation. Supporting that number of older and elderly people is an enormous drain on an economy. Furthermore, South Korea's birth-rate is way below the replacement rate. Its population is forecast to start shrinking from 2027. North Korea does not face these problems. Reunification will give South Korea a demographic rejuvenation. Table 5.1 succinctly sets out the problem – and the solution.

Table 5.1

	North Korea	South Korea
Population	23.3 million	49.0 million
% of population aged 65 or more	8.5%	9.6%
% aged 0–14	23.3%	18.3%
Median age	33.8	36.8
Total fertility rate (average no. of children per woman)	2.05	1.28
Sex ratio for those aged 15 and under (males/females)	1.03	1.106

Source: CIA World Factbook, 2007.

GDP per capita in South Korea (PPP basis) is now around US$24,200. In North Korea it's US$1,800. Not only does this starkly demonstrate the utter failure of communism as an economic model, it also provides another reason why South Korea needs reunification: labor costs in South Korea are now very high and, increasingly, South Korean companies are relocating their manufacturing outside Korea and particularly to nearby China. Labor costs will escalate further, given the absence of immigration of any significance and with the population dramatically ageing. Reunification will mean, overnight, abundant cheap labor for South Korean industry – not only cheap, but culturally homogeneous. Reunification will extend the time frame of South Korea's cost competitiveness by many decades. Of course, North Korea's infrastructure will need to be developed, but infrastructure, when done properly, has a habit of paying for itself. That is one reason why China's economy is so much more advanced than India's – China spends around seven times what India spends on infrastructure.

North and South

The leaders of North and South Korea held a historic summit in 2000 in which they agreed to greater dialogue and interaction. The South's then president Kim Dae Jung and the North's Kim Jong Il signed an accord that spoke of the "yearning for peaceful reunification of the fatherland." The propriety of the summit was later undermined when it emerged that South Korean conglomerate Hyundai had quietly sent US$500 million to Kim Jong Il to secure the summit. But the outcomes have remained intact – the two now cooperate more than at any other time.

While the US has been urging a total boycott of North Korea, South and North Korea were conducting many business, cultural, political, and even military exchanges by 2007. The two were considering a joint team for the 2008 Beijing Olympics. And in December 2006, they launched a bid to jointly host the 2014 Winter Olympics.

The two could reunify in the same way that East and West Germany did. However, the economic gap between them is far greater than it was between the two Germanys. The gap is growing. The South does not want reunification for several decades, believing that the cost would be prohibitive. Instead, current thinking is that North Korea should be economically transformed to a state where it is ready for reunification – or at least to a point where South Korea is ready to receive it. South Korea operates the Gaeseong Industrial Zone in North Korea as one means by which North Korea might be readied. It is expected to employ 700,000 workers and house 2,000 companies when it is completed in 2012. Should this materialize, then it alone will educate many North Koreans and their families about life outside North Korea – the wealth, the choices people have, and the opportunity. Currently, it employs 7,000 North Koreans and some 500 South Korean managers across 15 factories. South Korean companies have invested elsewhere in North Korea too, with South Korea's Reunification Ministry saying that such investment will help to develop North Korea so that North Koreans will not become "a displaced, misfortunate minority group" within a post-reunification Korea.[2]

South Korea has run a tourist resort in North Korea at Mount Geumgang since 1998. Around 1.5 million South Koreans have visited the resort to date. Hyundai operates the resort and it is believed to have sent around US$850 million in royalties to North Korea in return for being allowed to operate the resort.[3]

An enormous peace dividend will be earned from reunification. Both Koreas maintain enormous armies largely to balance out that of the other. North Korea alone has 1.1 million soldiers. Combining the two militaries will be a big task. It will involve a big reduction in servicemen too, thus releasing more manpower for the civilian workforce.

Another factor that will hamper North Korea's integration with South Korea is the technical backwardness of almost all North Koreans. Most simply have no idea of contemporary technology. The Australian Trade Commission, for example, even advises businesspeople traveling to North Korea to hand out printed matter – preferably in Korean – rather than videos or DVDs, as corporate ownership of VCR or DVD equipment is limited and affected by power shortages.

North Korean Backwardness

Censorship in North Korea is more thorough than anywhere. Educated North Koreans have no understanding of contemporary developments in the outside world, or any understanding of how backward their country is. The censorship is so total that when they are confronted with the truth, they are apt to assume that it is all lies.

Televisions and radios are hardwired to receive only government-controlled frequencies. Mobile phones were banned in 2004. Access to the Internet is banned totally. Most other dictatorships attempt to control the Internet by using filters and threatening service providers to block certain sites. But North Korea simply doesn't allow the Internet to operate at all within its borders. The designated North Korean web suffix ".kp" remains dormant. Some small de facto cybercafés have been allowed to open but they connect only to the country's closed network.[4]

North Korea was heavily dependent economically on the Soviet Union when the latter collapsed in 1990. At that time, much of its infrastructure including its power plants was already decades old and out of date. Black-outs are commonplace. Oil shortages have become severe too. Reportedly, the North has even tried to burn tires in its power plants to generate electricity. The capital Pyongyang has electricity for much of the day but most of the rest of the country does not.

One of the better known signs of North Korea's profound economic backwardness relates to nighttime satellite imaging of the Korean peninsular: the South is ablaze with light – from street lights, factories, offices and housing – out to sea Japan is also ablaze, and the North is one large black hole.

There are few cars and even intercity trucks and buses are increasingly rare. Nampo is the main port but, extraordinarily, there are no container cranes – containers must be hoisted using conventional cranes.

Famine occurs periodically. The worst was in 1995–99 when anywhere from 200,000 to 3 million North Koreans died. Foreign food aid was essential for preventing an even greater catastrophe. China and South Korea have been the North's two main sources of food aid.

Famine has had a devastating effect on the physical appearance of North Korean children. According to 2005 UN statistics, the average seven-year-old boy in North Korea is 18 centimeters shorter and nine kilograms lighter than his South Korean counterpart.[5]

Some economic reforms were introduced in 2002 – subsidies to state-owned enterprises were reduced, workers were to be paid according to what they produced, and private farmers' markets that had been tolerated were legalized and allowed to expand the range of goods on offer. These measures helped to reduce some of the rigidities in the economy.

Nonetheless, the government is chronically short of funds. Banking embargoes ensure that North Korea does not have access to the international banking system.

Strong evidence suggests that elements in the North Korean government have sought to raise funds either for their regime or for themselves or most probably both by smuggling narcotics; counterfeiting foreign currency, particularly US dollars; smuggling missiles; and counterfeiting and smuggling US brand cigarettes and pharmaceuticals such as Viagra.[6] In 2003, Australian authorities intercepted and impounded a North Korean freighter off the coast of Sydney that had earlier offloaded a consignment of 50 kilograms of heroin at an Australian port, providing firm evidence of one means by which the regime has attempted to raise cash.

Kim Jong Il

The slavish devotion to North Korea's founder Kim Il Sung demanded of North Koreans reduced them to a nation of children. One woman who died trying to rescue Kim family portraits from a burning school was elevated to national-hero status by the rigidly controlled state media. It was thought when Kim Il Sung was president that things could not get worse. But then his son Kim Jong Il became leader after his father's death in 1994 and they did. Whereas Kim senior appeared motivated by ideology, Kim junior is motivated by power and avarice. Accounts of his lifestyle are exaggerated probably but among the salacious details supplied by exiles who claim to have been close to him are that he has a collection of more than 100 imported limousines, he flies in restaurateurs from around the world to cook for him while North Koreans have been starving, and he travels with an entourage of women who are trained to service him sexually.[7]

Kim maintains power in North Korea with his "army first" policy, whereby the military and senior civil service receive far greater food rations than everyone else as well as other material privileges, thus helping to ensure their loyalty.

Kim Jong Il is in his sixties. The next leader is likely to be one of his sons. He has at least three. Apparently a family dynasty was expected. Kim Il Sung maintained that if he fell short of completing the revolution, then it would be continued by his son and his grandson.[8] Kim's eldest son was thought to be the heir apparent until he was arrested in 2001 as he tried to enter Japan using a fake Dominican Republic passport. The fact that he wasn't traveling with an entourage or even with security guards suggested that he was already out of favor. The purpose of the visit to Japan was to visit Tokyo Disneyland. Instead, the Japanese authorities arrested him and expelled him to China, causing his father to have to cancel an official visit to China due to the embarrassment of it all. And so the succession remains unclear.

Suggestions for Business Strategists and Scenario Developers

▶ Scenarios for South Korea need to take into account the possibility and effects of reunification with the North. Reunification will involve many costs for the South in terms of building the North's infrastructure and so on, but it will also have a dramatic demographic effect. No longer would Korea be the world's most rapidly ageing country, and labor competitiveness would be dramatically restored.

Notes

1 *Financial Times*, "Room for one more," July 8, 2006.
2 *International Herald Tribune*, "Koreans work at making unification real," July 19, 2006.
3 *The Economist*, "Testing times," October 28, 2006.
4 *International Herald Tribune*, "North Korea ranked 'worst Internet black hole,'" October 23, 2006.
5 *International Herald Tribune*, "North Korea cites bumper crop to shun food aid," October 7, 2005.
6 *International Herald Tribune*, "A hungry North Korea sends city people to farms," June 2, 2005.
7 Becker, J., *Rogue Regime: Kim Jong Il and the Looming Threat of North Korea*, Oxford University Press, 2005.
8 *International Herald Tribune*, "North Korea raises notion of a 3rd-generation Kim," February 1, 2005.

6

The Rush Out of India by Indian Companies

▷ India's biggest companies have announced dozens of M&A deals abroad. Why? Not because they want to show the world how powerful they are but because they want to diversify away from India.

▷ The desire for Indian business to diversify away from India will remain a powerful urge for as long as India remains a relatively unattractive place to do business even for homegrown businesses. So get set for a new phenomenon – the Indian multinational.

The phenomenon of Indian multinationals has only recently emerged. But is it a brief flash or a long-term trend? Definitely the latter. But this is no victory for Indian nationalism. Indian companies are diversifying away from India and with good reason.

For a long time, Indian companies were discouraged and even prevented from investing abroad. It had to do with maintaining India's highly interventionist exchange rate regime. It had some cultural underpinnings too. There has long been a suspicion of things foreign in India. Such a sentiment has cultural underpinnings: traditionally, Hindus lost their caste if they traveled across the sea. No longer would a Brahmin be considered a Brahmin if he or she traveled abroad, for example.

But the shackles, including rules on how much debt Indian companies can accrue, were loosened and in only a short period a stampede out of India erupted, helped by newfound profitability: average profit margins in India have been around 10% – more than twice the global average. This has allowed Indian firms to make more money than ever before. And so what are they doing with all this excess cash? To a large degree they are investing it abroad. According to one study, 60% of India's 200 biggest companies were looking to invest overseas by early 2007.[1]

The buying spree commenced in 2000 when Indian companies closed 50 foreign deals worth just less than US$1 billion. By 2006, US$23 billion was spent acquiring foreign firms, more than five times the previous record and certainly far more than foreigners spent acquiring Indian companies, and involved around 170 deals. And in the first three months of 2007 alone, Indian firms announced 34 foreign takeovers worth a total of US$10.7 billion.[2] And all this, when the Indian economy was supposedly growing at around 8% per annum. That so many Indian companies still wanted to diversify out of India is instructive about the true state of the Indian economy despite the headline growth rate.

Tata Group has been India's biggest investor abroad. It now operates in 55 countries and generates around 35% of its revenue outside India. In 2001, it bought the UK tea company Tetley for US$432 million. In 2004, it paid US$289 million for Singapore's NatSteel, US$130 million for Tyco Global Network of the US, and US$102 million for South Korea's Daewoo Commercial Vehicle Company. In 2005, it paid around US$120 million for UK engineering and design firm Incat Technologies, and US$239 for Bermuda-based wholesale telecommunications company Teleglobe. It bought the Eight O'Clock Coffee brand in 2006 for US$220 million, making Tata the biggest seller of whole bean coffee in the US. It also bought a 30% stake in Glaceau of the US, a maker of flavored water, for US$677 million. In early 2007, Tata Steel paid US$11.3 billion for London-based Corus, a European steel group formed in 1999 by the merger of British Steel with the Netherlands-based Koninklijke Hoogovens.

Other notable foreign acquisitions include:

- Videocon paid US$288 million for the picture tube business of France's Thompson in 2005.
- Indian drug maker Dr Reddy bought Germany's Betapharm for US$572 million in 2006.
- Ranbaxy paid US$372 million for Romania's Terapia in 2006.
- India's Oil and Natural Gas Corp. bought a US$1.4 billion stake in Brazil's Petrobras in 2006.
- Suzlon Energy paid US$565 million for Hansen, a Belgian gearbox maker, in 2006. It made a US$1.3 billion bid in early 2007 for Repower, a German turbine maker.

- India's biggest aluminum producer Hindalco Industries, part of the Aditya Birla Group, made a US$6 billion bid for Canada's Novelis, in early 2007.

- India's United Spirits paid US$1.19 billion for Scottish whisky maker Whyte & Mackay in mid-2007.

- India's Sun Pharmaceutical Industries agreed to buy Israel's Taro Pharmaceutical Industries for US$454 million.

Management consultants McKinsey estimate that 60–70% of cross-border takeovers fail.[3] The odds for Indian companies succeeding abroad might well be worse, given cultural and other differences. They are not at the cutting edge of modern management. Nor do they have much expertise at managing assets abroad. Many of India's industrialists have become big in India because of their ties to government officials. These connections have afforded them licensing and other privileges that have shielded them from open competition. They do not enjoy this sort of protection abroad. Indian companies might even repeat the pattern of Japanese investment in the West in the 1980s, when Japanese companies overreached themselves by paying too much for too many US and European companies.

Nationalism vs Rationalism

The Indian media greeted each major acquisition abroad by an Indian company as a big win for Indian pride. India erupted with a wave of jubilation when Tata Group bought Corus in early 2007. India was striking back at the former colonialists suggested the headlines. Many in India saw this and other takeovers of Western companies as part of a satisfying reversal of fortune. Indians were jubilant again when Hindalco Industries made its US$6 billion bid for Canada's Novelis. One of Novelis's customers was Coca-Cola, for which it makes cans. "The cans that people drink Coca-Cola in will be made by an Indian company," trumpeted the *Times of India*.[4] Apparently, that's important. The possibility that Indian companies are at least in part deserting India was barely considered.

Nor does nationalism help to justify high price–earnings ratios. When Hindalco's bid was announced, its shares fell 14%: Novelis is a higher cost producer of aluminum than Hindalco and it was also laden with debt and loss making. Similarly, when Tata Steel finally won control of Corus for US$11.3 billion, the markets did not rejoice. Instead, shares in Tata Steel fell almost 11%.[5]

India, long aggrieved at colonialism and other affronts, seems to suffer from a collective inferiority complex. And so, putting it bluntly, perceived successes over the "white" man are celebrated and exalted. And when there is failure and loss, then that is because India has somehow been cheated or tricked.

Indians are very proud – justifiably so on many counts. But it also leads to hyperbole. A nationwide survey conducted in India in July 2006 by the Chicago Council on Global Affairs found that respondents ranked India as the second most influential country in the world after the US, and more influential than the EU, Great Britain, France, China, Germany, Japan, and Russia.[6] When asked to rank the US, Japan, South Korea, Germany, China, and India in terms of their leadership in developing new technologies and products, the respondents ranked the US as the most innovative but with India a close second. What needs to be remembered is that Indian companies might be desperate to invest abroad but foreign companies are not showing a similar desperation to invest in India.

Why the Rush?

Why do so many Indian companies want to invest outside India? Because doing business in India isn't easy. The rule of law is weak and India's courts slow and unreliable. Government policies often are watered down if implemented at all, making the business environment unpredictable. Privatization has been slow. For example, plans to privatize the airports of New Delhi and Mumbai and thus inject badly needed capital into them have been stalled for years, with thousands of airport workers striking and picketing both airports. India has a big population but few are well skilled and English is not as widely spoken as most people think.

Those sectors that have put in stellar performances – IT particularly – have done well because they are not particularly engaged with India. Indian IT companies' customers largely are abroad, their output is exported via computer terminals and telephone wires and not through India's appalling ports. Their output is also largely invisible to the eye and so harder for Indian bureaucrats to intrude upon, ask for bribes, and so on. Nor do they rely so much on India's infrastructure. What they do rely upon are India's people, or at least the thin top layer that is educated and typically can speak English.

And as cutting edge and innovative as India's IT and back-office outsourcing sector is, it accounts for around a million jobs, or less than one-quarter of 1% of India's workforce.[7] Against this is the fact that India has the world's biggest population of adult illiterates – around 312 million – more than the entire population of the US. India might have enjoyed five minutes of economic sunshine but there are still plenty of shadows.

Why else might India's own companies want to diversify away from India? For all the reasons why India remains relatively unattractive to foreign investors:

- India still spends comparatively little on infrastructure. It spends far less than China, for example. One estimate is that for every $1 that India spends, China is spending $7.[8]

- Indian democracy means that policymaking is short term and not farsighted. On the other hand, policymaking in China is the opposite.

- Most Indians remain very poor. The World Bank estimates that half of India's 1.1 billion people live on less than US$2 a day.

- Foreigners are still blocked from directly investing in many sectors and where they can invest, the licensing is prohibitive and the risk that government policy might be quickly reversed is always present.

- Privatization is lethargic. India is one of the few countries on earth where communists are in government in many areas, including in the Congress-led coalition national government that came to power in 2004.

- The price mechanism works poorly due to a complex array of food and gasoline subsidies.

- Airports and airlines are in an abysmal state. At the start of 2006, all of India's airlines owned fewer than 200 jets.[9]

- Around 60% of the labor force comprises rural workers.

- Labor laws in India (of which there are many) are restrictive. Manufacturing workers cannot put in more than 54 hours of overtime in any three-month period even if they want to earn the extra money. In any event, overtime pay is twice the normal pay.

- It takes an average of 85 hours to load and reload a ship at India's major ports – 10 times longer than in Hong Kong or Singapore.[10]

- By late 2008, around 25% of world container ship capacity will comprise vessels of at least 6,000 twenty-foot equivalent units (TEUs), but India does not yet have a single port capable of handling such a ship.[11]

- India has some of the world's highest rail costs – transporting one TEU one kilometer in India is 53% more expensive than in the US.[12]

- India remains intrinsically hostile to foreign brands. In 2006, five Indian states banned the sale of Pepsi and Coca-Cola after a New Delhi-based research group claimed to have found unacceptable levels of pesticides in the soft drinks. No other body was able to replicate the results. And yet the water that comes out of the public mains in any Indian city or town is severely contaminated with all manner of pollutants but little fuss is made about that.

■ Distribution is so poor that an estimated 40% of farm produce in India perishes between the farm and reaching the consumer.[13]

By the mid-2000s, India's economy was doing well, but then what economy wasn't? But then India's economy was growing from a low base. World Bank data even showed that when ranking the world's economies by their average GDPs for the five-year period 1980–84 with that for 2001–05, India's position among the world's economies actually fell one notch, meaning that for the periods examined, India was doing little better than the average and worse than many.[14]

Another grave problem is getting enough staff with management and leadership abilities to run good companies in India. India does have its celebrated Indian Institutes of Technology but they produce only around 4,000 graduates a year, a pitiful number for a country with a billion-plus population (see Chapter 11). Indian companies do not face such critical professional staff shortages when they invest abroad.

Capital Drain

India's infrastructure remains abysmal. But even though it remains a capital-scarce economy, FDI out of India is skyrocketing. Acquisitions overseas by Indian companies have been funded partly by bond issues or loans raised abroad. Even so, in March 2007, India's Associated Chambers of Commerce and Industry (ASSOCHAM) said that it expected FDI outflow for the year to be US$15 billion, and FDI inflow to be US$12 billion. This meant that the money that Indian companies were taking out of India to invest overseas was greater than what India was getting back from foreigners directly investing in India. And so in the FDI stakes, India in 2007 was a net loser.[15] But the Indian media remain triumphant.

The contrast with China could hardly be greater. By 2007, it was earning around US$6 billion in FDI every single month, far more than what Chinese companies were investing abroad.

Will India's big companies cease investing abroad? Not now, unless they run out of money or at least the ability to raise money. Indian companies now have the means to diversify away from India and all its business complexities. It is a sensible and prudent strategy. The age of the Indian multinational is here to stay, particularly if the Indian economy remains as beset by corruption, red tape, and poor infrastructure as it currently is, while India's competitors improve. Indian companies are voting with their feet.

Suggestions for Business Strategists and Scenario Developers

▶ Would-be investors in India should take note of where cashed-up Indian companies themselves are choosing to invest – increasingly it's not in India.

▶ The eagerness of Indian companies to invest outside India means that those in developed markets with assets to sell should consider marketing those assets in India.

▶ However, scenario planners cannot dismiss the possibility that, in the future, public opinion in India will shift from seeing acquisitions abroad by Indian companies as a triumph to a rejection of India and the Indian government responding with new obstacles to slow down the outflow of investment.

Notes

1 *The Economist*, "Marauding maharajahs," March 31, 2007.
2 Ibid.
3 Ibid.
4 *Financial Times*, "Takeover bid knocks Hindalco shares," February 13, 2007.
5 *Business Times*, "Tata Steel beats CSN to acquire Corus," February 1, 2007.
6 The Chicago Council of Global Affairs, "Global Views 2006: India Public Topline Report," September, 2006.
7 *The Age*, "China and India: Not quite tigers," November 21, 2005.
8 *International Herald Tribune*, "The next industrial giant is … India?," September 1, 2006.
9 *International Herald Tribune*, "To fly high, India must modernize its airports," December 8, 2005.
10 *Business Times*, "India's US$320b road, rail plan may fail to draw funds," October 10, 2006.
11 *Business Times*, "Poor facilities, high port costs curb India's growth," September 19, 2006.
12 Ibid.
13 *International Herald Tribune*, "In India, mom and pop get shoved aside," October 20, 2006.
14 *The Economist*, "Economy rankings," December 16, 2006.
15 *Business Times*, "India's FDI outflows set to beat inflows," March 20, 2007.

Asia's Nuclear Future

▷ 70% of the energy in China comes from coal. Worldwide the figure is 25%.

▷ 16% of all power generated worldwide comes from nuclear sources. In China the figure is 2.0%. In India it's 2.8%.

▷ China's demand for uranium will jump tenfold in the foreseeable future.

▷ Half the world's nuclear reactors will be in Asia by 2030.

The economies of China and India are growing fast. Neither produces enough power even for existing requirements. And the power that is produced comes largely from the dirtiest, most harmful means possible: burning coal. The situation is unsustainable. Nuclear power is an obvious solution and so probably by 2030, Asia will be home to at least half of the world's nuclear reactors.

Rocketing Power Demand

China and India account for two-fifths of the world's population. But they do not use anything like two-fifths of the world's energy. The gap suggests the massive potential for growth in demand for power in these two economies. Existing capacity is insufficient even to supply current needs and regular power cuts are a way of life in both countries. With their growing economies, the US government's National Intelligence Council has estimated that India's energy consumption will at least double by 2020. China's will rise by even more, by 150%.[1]

Already both are big net importers of energy. And the energy import bill is only going to escalate. India's economy is smaller than China's but it is even more dependent on imported energy. Its government has forecast that with average annual economic growth of 6%, the share of imported oil consumed in India will rise from 70% in 2005 to 86% in 2025.[2] Others have forecast that by then India will need to import practically all its energy needs. India's current share of world oil demand is about 3%. By 2025, it will be nearer 10%.

China is rich in energy resources in absolute terms. Unlike India, it does have vast coal reserves and significant oil and gas reserves. But it is not rich in per capita terms. Proven oil reserves represent just 2.2% of the world's total reserves, and this when China has 22% of the world's population. China's major oilfields in eastern China, which account for 90% of total crude production, have peaked and are in decline. Gas reserves are even smaller and account for less than 1% of the world's known reserves.[3] Consumption of oil and gas outstrips domestic production and the gaps between the two are growing ever wider. China started to import significant amounts of natural gas in 2006. By 2020, it will import 30% of its gas needs and at least 60% of its oil needs.[4]

And this when the international competition for energy grows ever more intense. The UK, for example, became a net gas importer in 2004. And in 2005, Indonesia became a net oil importer, which is particularly disconcerting given that Indonesia is actually a member of OPEC.

Part of the problem is that energy is not priced efficiently. For example, kerosene, which is used by the poorer households in India for cooking, heating, and lighting, is sold at well below the market price. Any government that attempts to substantially alter this can expect to lose the next election. This means that inefficient energy pricing is an almost intractable problem. Similarly, electricity supplied to houses across China is too cheaply priced. Power theft is another problem. Illegal, nonmetered links to the public grid are commonplace in both countries. And even more power is lost through inefficient and outmoded transmission. But even if these problems are fixed, the demand for power will still dramatically outstrip supply in future years unless substantial new capacity is installed.

Asia's Nuclear Reactors

Both countries are seeking to diversify their power sources. Both are building gas-fired stations and China has embarked on massive hydroelectric schemes. But they are not enough. Another source is nuclear power.

According to the World Nuclear Association, 285 nuclear reactors were operational, under construction, planned or proposed for South and East Asia at the start of 2007. And of the 442 operational reactors in the world, almost a quarter, or 109, were in Asia. Another 28 were under construction worldwide, of which 15 were in Asia.[5]

Within South and East Asia, China had 10 (with another 5 under construction), India 16 (7 more under construction), Japan 55 (1), South Korea 20 (0), Pakistan 2 (1), and Taiwan 6 (2). The most nuclear of Asia's economies were South Korea, Japan, and Taiwan, which generated 45%, 29% and 20% respectively of their power from nuclear sources. China's nuclear power plants generated 2% of its power and India 2.8%.[6] Vietnam has no nuclear power plants at present but is developing plans for its first nuclear power plant ahead of when it shifts from being a small net oil exporter to a new importer around 2014. Worldwide, nuclear power accounts for 16% of all the power generated.

Politically, some in the West might see advantage in Asia turning to nuclear power. After all, the bulk of the world's oil reserves are in the Middle East and in the hands of regimes that are either politically unstable, Islamic or both. Many are not reliable friends of the West. And no doubt there are lawmakers in the US who are mindful that most of the world's oil reserves are controlled by Muslims but that Christians control most of the world's uranium reserves. Raising the world's reliance on uranium-generated power will be one way to tip the power balance back in favor of the West. Otherwise more deals, such as the multibillion-dollar oil and gas deals in 2004 that both India and China struck with Iran against the wishes of the US, are likely.

No doubt such thinking played a role in the US decision to sign a nuclear cooperation treaty with India in 2006 even though India is not a signatory to the Nuclear Non-proliferation Treaty. And the US government's Export–Import Bank provided US firm Westinghouse with US$5 billion in loan guarantees in respect of its bids to supply technology for the construction of nuclear power plants in China's Guangdong and Zhejiang provinces.

Another factor that will drive China's embrace of uranium is that its efforts to buy oil assets abroad have on occasion been thwarted. In 2005, for example, the attempt by the China National Offshore Oil Company

(CNOOC) to pay almost US$20 billion for US oil company Unocal was struck down by the US Congress. Among the concerns was that China's control of Unocal would give it greater political leverage in countries where Unocal has interests. The US views oil as a "strategic commodity." And a former CIA director said that the US should not allow oil owned by a US company to end up in the hands of a "potential enemy."[7]

A Nuclear China

So what are China's current plans to go nuclear? China plans a fivefold increase in its nuclear power-generating capacity from 2006 to 2020. By 2006, China had 10 nuclear reactors. Five more were under construction, 13 more were planned and a further 50 had been proposed, meaning that by the end of 2006, China expected to have at least 78 nuclear reactors in the foreseeable future. Such growth promises to be big business for foreign contractors. In early 2007, for example, China awarded Areva of France a contract to build two nuclear reactors in Guangdong province. The Toshiba unit Westinghouse Electric was awarded a contract to build two nuclear reactors in Shandong province. Each contract for two reactors was worth around US$5 billion.[8]

Assuming that each new plant will consume the same uranium as the average of the existing plants (in fact, the newer plants are likely to consume more), then China's annual demand for uranium will rise to at least 10,093 tons, from the current 1,294 tons. China produces about half its current uranium needs, suggesting that almost all its future requirements will be imported.

Currently, probably most of the uranium that China imports comes from Kazakhstan, Russia, and Namibia. We don't actually know as the data is withheld by China. Certainly, Kazakhstan is the world's fourth biggest producer of uranium and currently supplies about 8% of world demand.[9] Australia signed an agreement with China in 2006 to supply it with uranium for use in its nuclear power plants. (Australia has 40% of the world's known uranium reserves. Canada is the next biggest source.) Part of the agreement was that China would not use Australian uranium in its weapons program or for other military purposes. China is also a signatory to the Nuclear Non-proliferation Treaty. In any event, analysts believed that China already had all the fissile nuclear material it needed for weapons and so there was little reason for Australian uranium to be used for anything other than civilian purposes.[10]

In addition, China's main nuclear power plant operator, the Chinese National Nuclear Corp., was involved with the 2006 float of UraniumSA, an Australian-based uranium exploration company. Its Australian representative was given a nonexecutive seat on the board.[11] The company will look for uranium in South Australia, the Australian state that is home to three of Australia's four existing uranium mines. (It was also the source of the uranium used for the nuclear bombs that were dropped on Hiroshima and Nagasaki in 1945.)

An Atomic India

And India's plans? India's current long-term plan is to increase nuclear power output to 25–30% of total power output by 2050. As at 2006, India expected to have 47 nuclear reactors in the foreseeable future, all owned and operated by the state-owned Nuclear Power Corporation of India. Again, assuming that each new plant consumes the same uranium as the average of existing plants, then India's annual demand for uranium will be 3,918 tons, up from 1,334 tons. Currently, India is self-sufficient in uranium. Eventually it will become a net importer.

Assistance for India's new nuclear plants will come in part from the US, which, as mentioned, signed a nuclear cooperation agreement with India in early 2006, reversing 30 years of nonproliferation policy. The agreement allows for the US to cooperate with India's civilian nuclear program, even though India is not a signatory to the Nuclear Nonproliferation Treaty.

Given that India has far less energy reserves than China, and must import a greater proportion of its needs, and that it does have some native reserves of uranium, it actually faces an even greater incentive than China to increase its nuclear power capacity. The endorsement of its nuclear program by the US will pave the way for other Western governments and companies to provide technical and other assistance.

Coal and Catastrophe

But the greatest imperative to go nuclear comes from pollution. The bulk of China's power is produced by burning coal, a particularly environmentally harmful means. But doesn't China have the right to industrialize just as Western economies have? The main difference is that China depends overwhelmingly on coal. Western economies do not. In fact, China currently uses 40% of all the coal that is extracted in the world – more than the US, all of Europe and Japan put together.[12] Coal burning accounts for around 70% of the energy produced in China against a global average of around 25%.[13] China wants to get this figure down to 60% by 2020, but even if such a reduction is possible, it will actually mean that coal-generated power will dramatically increase in absolute terms.

Coal is used so extensively because it is one energy source that China does have abundant supplies of. Shanxi province is China's main coal-producing province. The reliance on coal is not abating. In 2005 alone, consumption increased by 14% over the previous year. According to one report, a new coal-fired power station was opening somewhere in China every 7–10 days.[14] According to another, China builds new power-generating capacity almost equivalent to the UK's entire stock every year and most of it is coal-fired.[15] Every sector of the economy was hungry for more power. Industrial production alone was rising by 16% annually.[16]

And the result? China leads the world in sulfur dioxide emissions, which cause acid rain. It has quickly become one of the most polluted countries on earth. Air quality is abysmal in many areas. Those who have been to the capital Beijing will have experienced being able to literally wipe the grime off their skin after spending little more than a few hours outdoors. Official estimates are that 400,000 Chinese die each year from diseases related to air pollution. Separately, the World Bank says that 16 of the world's 20 most polluted cities are in China.[17]

The increase in global warming gases from China's coal use is projected to exceed that for all industrialized countries combined over the next 25 years, exceeding by five times the reduction in emissions called for by the 1997 Kyoto Protocol.[18]

Pollution levels in India are rising too but the problem is not as acute as in China. Nonetheless, India too is stepping up its construction of coal-fired plants, meaning that its greenhouse gas emissions will also accelerate. And given that India's population is expected to pass that of China's in 2030, that's a worrying trend. Alternative sources of fuel must be found. Natural gas is one. Another is nuclear fuel.

Almost a quarter of all the world's nuclear power plants are in Asia. Probably by 2030, it will be half, the bulk of which will be in China and India. There might be uneasiness now about their nuclear programs, but if their use of fossil fuels continues to grow exponentially, then it may not be long before the world actually begs China and India to build more nuclear reactors.

Suggestions for Business Strategists and Scenario Developers

▶ Mining companies involved in uranium exploration and extraction, particularly those in Australia and Canada, will be big winners from growing nuclear power generation in Asia. So too will suppliers of nuclear technology and know-how. Specialized services associated with transporting nuclear fuel, monitoring its use, maintaining nuclear reactors, and treating spent fuel will all offer big fee-generating opportunities. The sector will also need specialized translation services for highly technical reports and manuals.

Notes

1 National Intelligence Council, *Mapping the Global Future*, US government, 2004.
2 *Financial Times*, "India bids high to catch up," February 25, 2005.
3 Strecker Downs, E., *China's Quest for Energy Security*, Rand, 2000.
4 Ibid.
5 World Nuclear Association, "World nuclear power reactors 2005–06 and uranium requirements," August 15, 2006.
6 Ibid.
7 *Business Times*, "CNOOC seen upping Unocal offer to US$19b," July 15, 2005.
8 *International Herald Tribune*, "China to award deal on reactors to Areva," March 6, 2007.
9 Backman, M., *Inside Knowledge: Streetwise in Asia*, Palgrave Macmillan, 2005, p. 59.
10 *International Herald Tribune*, "China to buy Australian uranium," April 3, 2006.
11 *The Age*, "Chinese join the uranium search," September 5, 2006.
12 *The Economist*, "Anti-hero," September 9, 2007.
13 *China Daily*, "Growing energy demand plaguing China," August 12, 2004.
14 *International Herald Tribune*, "China's burning coal casts a global cloud," June 12, 2006.
15 *The Economist*, "The heat is on," September 9, 2006.
16 *The Economist*, "Industrial production," September 3, 2005.
17 BBC News, "China's dirty energy takes its toll," November 9, 2004.
18 *International Herald Tribune*, "China's burning coal casts a global cloud," June 12, 2006.

Water Wars

8

> ▷ China has 22% of the world's population but only 8% of its fresh water.
>
> ▷ Just 14.8% of China is arable but 48.8% of India is.
>
> ▷ China's current plans for water engineering are worth more than US$200 billion.
>
> ▷ Rice prices in Asia are set to escalate significantly.

Asia's populations are not just getting bigger, they're getting richer. This means that not only will Asia consume more water but more water per capita. But there is a problem: the absolute quantity of fresh water in Asia is falling. The problem will be especially acute in China and Indonesia. And in India, the real challenge will be urban water sanitation. The growing scarcity of this most basic of commodities must be factored into any scenario building for Asia's future.

Distribution is a big problem. Ageing pipes laid down during the colonial era in many Asian countries have not been well maintained. About 40% of the water that's distributed in New Delhi, for example, simply leaks away.[1] Very often no water comes out of the taps of even middle-class areas, leaving housewives to dial for private water companies to bring water to their houses by truck. River water in most Indian cities is polluted with runoff and discharge from factories, religious offerings, and ashes from cremation grounds.

But it's not just about fresh water distribution. If the distribution of fresh water is replete with loss and leakage, there's no reason to assume that leakage is any less of a problem when it comes to sewage in Asia's cities. Not only that, but the vast majority of Asia's sewage is not treated. It is simply emptied into river systems or piped out to sea in its raw state. Even in seemingly pristine waters such as those surrounding Bali's southern seashore, raw effluent is pumped into the sea. The seawater along Bali's resort strip has been found to have extraordinarily high levels of coliform and E. coli bacteria.

The problems of water and effluent are being compounded by massive internal migration from rural to urban areas. In China, the millions who have left the countryside to find work in the cities in the past two decades represent the biggest mass migration in history. The problem is growing in India too. Mumbai, for example, is forecast to have a population of 28.5 million people by 2020. Around 1,500 people arrive to live in the city each day.[2]

China to Spend Billions

China faces Asia's most serious water challenges. It expects to have a critical water shortage by 2030 when its population is forecast to have reached 1.6 billion. The Ministry of Water Resources has calculated that by then China will need between 130 and 230 million cubic meters of water more per year than at present.

One problem is that China is surprisingly arid. China makes up around 22% of the world's population but has around 8% of the world's renewable fresh water. Much of its grain is grown in the north but most of its water is in the south. The mismatch is worsening. The northern plain, which is home to around 400 million people, produces about a quarter of China's grain but the aquifer beneath it is falling by 1.5 meters a year. Already some 400 major cities face water shortages and restrictions. But China's water is getting more polluted too. Almost 60% of the more than 400 sites along China's seven main rivers that were monitored for water quality in 2004 were found to be too polluted for human consumption.[3]

Importantly, China's government does recognize that it has a serious problem. Various ministries have developed plans that will cost billions of dollars to alleviate the problems. Herein lie huge opportunities for foreign participants such as water engineering contractors and the like.

The Ministry of Construction announced in 2006 a plan to spend almost US$126 billion by 2010 on waste water treatment plants and upgrading water distribution systems.[4] Foreign companies such as Veolia Environment and Suez, both of France, had already been awarded big contracts in this sector in China and could expect more. Suez, in partnership with

Hong Kong's New World Developments, was awarded a 50-year contract in 2002 to pipe water to more than 850,000 residents in Chongqing, in partnership with the city government, for example. It expected to soon have 20 similar joint ventures around China.[5]

A separate proposal from a competing ministry calls for a huge engineering scheme to divert water from the south to the north via three massive canals thousands of kilometers long, thereby shifting 50 billion cubic meters of water northwards each year. The estimated cost will be US$60 billion. The first water to reach the north via the scheme is scheduled to do so in 2010. But the entire scheme is not scheduled for completion until 2050.[6] Environmentalists are critical and undoubtedly such a scheme would be hugely distorting to wetlands, wildlife, and the water table.

Another proposal would see water diverted from Tibet to northern China via a series of aqueducts, tunnels, and reservoirs. The proposal calls for a partly underground 300 kilometer waterway to be constructed to send up to 8 billion cubic meters of water a year from the Jinsha and other rivers in the Tibetan region. They would then be fed into the Yellow River's upper reaches. The proposal entails enormous environmental concerns, and huge cost. To date, it remains a proposal only; no starting date has been announced.[7]

And along China's coastal areas, where urbanization and rapid industrial growth are putting much pressure on fresh water supplies, the plan is to construct a series of desalination plants that can convert seawater to drinking water. Authorities hope that these will account for 16–24% of the water supply in the coastal areas by 2010.[8]

Water treatment and sewage disposal are other areas ripe for investment. Between 2000 and 2006 more than 1,000 waste water treatment plants were built in China. And while many cities have overinvested in the plants they have underinvested in sewage capacity. According to China's Ministry of Construction, the average utilization rate of China's waste water treatment plants is about 60% and about 50 plants in 30 cities operate at less than 30% capacity. Some plants do not operate at all. The problem is not so much that there is not enough sewage to be treated but that there are insufficient pipelines to carry sewage to the plants. Still, it remains the case that over a third of China's 660 cities do not have any water treatment facilities and nationally, only 56% of urban waste water is thought to be treated.[9]

The schemes are huge, complex, and competing. There is much work to be done at the provincial and municipal levels too. But importantly, there is recognition within government in China that there is a huge amount of work to be done. Real plans are being drawn up and big funds are being allocated. It all means genuine opportunities for outside contractors. Other Asian governments such as those in India face similar problems but are showing less resolve to find solutions.

India, Indonesia, and Singapore

India is in a better position water-wise than China, at least on the face of it. Just 14.8% of China is arable land but 48.8% of India is. Water contamination is a big issue in India. Industrial pollutants are becoming more of a problem as the country industrializes, as is pollution from households. Only about 10% of all sewage in India is treated. The rest, from both urban and industrial sources, is mostly poured into India's waterways.

New Delhi again provides a good example of what is happening in India's cities. Almost a quarter of Delhi households rely on ground wells for their water, in part or in whole.[10] And a quarter have no access to piped water and, among those that do, more than a quarter receive water for less than three hours each day. Nearly two million households do not have a toilet.

Most of the city's water supply comes from the Yamuna River which flows through it. The river originates in the Himalayas and arrives at New Delhi in a relatively clean state. It leaves laden with filth. Almost 900 million liters a day is extracted by the Delhi water board to be pumped into the city's water system. In return, the city's residents pour into it around 3,500 million liters of raw sewage. A government audit in 2005 found that the level of fecal coliform in the Yamuna was 100,000 times the level considered safe for bathing.

And in Indonesia, Asia's third most populous country, the quality of water stocks is also diminishing. Indonesia has one of the worst rates of sewage and sanitation coverage. Few Indonesian cities possess even minimal sanitation systems. Fewer than 3% of Jakarta's residents are connected to a sewer system, for example.[11] Many households rely on private septic tanks or they dispose of their waste directly into rivers and canals. Many and probably most households in Jakarta also rely on private wells and pumps for their water. But because the sewerage system is so poor, most of the groundwater is contaminated. A 2001 study, for example, found that 90% of Jakarta's shallow wells were polluted by domestic waste. Wells are dug indiscriminately, near tips and even cemeteries that sprawl throughout central Jakarta. Accordingly, the city faces repeated epidemics of gastrointestinal infections.

Poor controls on industry and enforcement of controls mean that Indonesia's water stocks also face serious industrial pollution. Excessive use of agricultural fertilizers and chemicals is another contributor. And again, due to poor controls and corruption that encourages regulators to look the other way, Indonesia's mining sector is increasingly a source of water pollution.

Singapore is one of the few countries in Asia with world-class water supplies. Of course, that's partly because Singapore is so small – the logistics are not as nightmarish compared with sprawling cities like Jakarta, Bangkok, or Delhi. Still, water in Singapore is priced sensibly, is clean and can be drunk straight from the tap, and loss from leakage is very small, about 5%. Water comes from several sources: local catchment areas, piped in from Malaysia, and from treating and reusing used water (so-called "New Water"). The city-state's first desalination plant was brought into commission in 2005 – a US$127 million reverse-osmosis plant that provides about 10% of Singapore's fresh water needs.[12] And so, as mentioned, Singapore water engineering companies are now looking to undertake work across Asia. An industry association, the Singapore Water Association, was formed in 2005 to facilitate the process.

Inefficient Water Markets

A big part of the problem is that water is underpriced throughout Asia. Low, negligible, or even no charging means that it is used wastefully; users tend to value commodities according to what they pay for them. In Delhi, for example, consumers pay no more than 40% of the actual cost of the water that is piped to them.[13]

Its distribution also tends to be handled by government authorities, which means that even if a sensible pricing regime is put in place, many customers pay less than they should by bribing officials to have their bills reduced. This happens with power too. Another problem is pilferage from the distribution system and, as mentioned, leakage caused by underinvestment in the distribution infrastructure.

Inefficient use of farming land also causes problems with water salinity. Again, this often has to do with pricing distortions. Farmers might receive subsidies on fertilizers, which means that marginal land is cultivated. Or they do not have proper title to the land that they use, giving them less incentive to manage it properly. Also, water is diverted to marginal land, causing natural lakes and underground aquifers to dry up. The problem is compounded as agricultural land is lost to urban expansion, factories, and even golf courses. Inefficient pricing for timber and illegal logging are also seeing many important water catchment areas across Asia disappear.

Also, polluters rarely pay for the mess they create, and as India and China industrialize, the amount of pollution has expanded exponentially, damaging water stocks. Yet again, this is a pricing problem. The price of pollution is free; the cost is not.

So a big part of Asia's water challenge will be to corporatize water supply and treatment services, and introduce market forces in a sector that traditionally is not seen by consumers as an arena for the market. "Why should I pay for something that falls from the sky," might be a common view. But encouraging consumers to use water more carefully is something that must be done if Asia is to avert some very serious shortages in the coming decades. The best way to do this is via appropriate pricing, which must be enforced. Quite simply, people must pay more for water everywhere.

Rocketing Rice Prices?

Perhaps the most overt consequence of growing water shortages in Asia will be felt in the prices that consumers must pay for the region's staple grain: rice. Nearly 460 million tons of rice is consumed globally each year – around 135 million tons of it by China and 84 million tons by India. Together, they accounted for 52% of total world consumption in 2004. By way of comparison, only 3.6 million tons of rice was consumed in the US in 2004.[14]

So China is the world's biggest consumer of rice. It will get bigger too as its population grows. But domestic rice production has been either flat or falling in recent years and the land available for rice production has been significantly falling.

Only about 6–7% of total world rice production is currently traded internationally. Of this, the market leader is Thailand, which accounted for 38% of world rice exports in 2004. The three biggest importers of rice currently are Indonesia, Bangladesh, and sub-Saharan Africa. The Philippines is also a big importer. (The three biggest exporters are Thailand, Vietnam, and India. The US and Australia are not as big but they export a far higher proportion of their crops as domestic demand is relatively low. In recent years, 45% of the US crop has been exported.)

China is not yet a big importer. But as the land available for rice cultivation shrinks and domestic production falls, China will become more important as a rice importer. This is when world rice inventories had approached a 26-year low by 2006.[15] Worldwide, the problem is that although rice yields have been rising, they have not been rising as fast as demand.

Desertification is one problem for China's rice output. One estimate is that China's deserts swallow around 3,600 square kilometers each year and now cover 18% of the country.[16] Desertification not only contributes to the loss of arable land but also to soil erosion and the silting up of rivers and dams.

Land is being reforested to try to slow the spread of desert. But this too is contributing to the decline in the land available for rice cultivation. Overall, China lost around 8 million hectares or 6.6% of its arable land between 1995 and 2005, according to China's Ministry of Land and Resources.[17]

A mitigating factor is that as developing country populations grow richer, they tend to substitute away from rice. This will help to alleviate the upwards pressure on the price of rice. But then China's population overall is not static. It is growing and is likely to continue to grow at least until 2030.

The Chinese might substitute away from rice on a per capita basis but not grain. Wheat and barley consumption will rise. It's unlikely that China will be able to produce all that will be needed. By one calculation, if per capita Chinese grain consumption grows to match that of Europe, then China will need almost 40% of today's world grain harvest.[18] But even if there is some substitution away from rice, the absolute level of rice consumption is likely to rise and rice imports will definitely rise. This has implications not just for China but for other rice-importing countries such as Indonesia and the Philippines. Clearly, a greater proportion of the world's rice that is produced will be internationally traded in coming years. Additional transport costs will add to the price of rice that consumers face but so too will additional demand in the face of declining regional supply.

Another source of pressure on food prices will come from the rise in demand for agricultural commodities from biofuel users, particularly as energy prices continue to remain at historic highs. Biofuel demand is a new demand that simply wasn't present a decade ago.

How Serious?

Some predict that water is likely to become so scarce in Asia relative to demand that it's only a matter of time before countries will go to war over water. Certainly, the nature of water means that underground aquifers, rivers, and lakes tend to cross national boundaries. Taking too much water upstream in one country can ruin the livelihoods of farmers downstream in a neighboring country, for example.

The two Indian states of Karnataka, where the IT center of Bangalore is located, and Tamil Nadu both draw water from the Cauvery River, for example. A 1991 court order demanding that Karnataka release 205 billion cubic feet of water from the Cauvery River to Tamil Nadu sparked riots against ethnic Tamils in Bangalore leaving more than eighteen people dead.[19] And again in early 2007 when a court made a similar ruling, many Bangalore businesses and schools closed temporarily out of fear of similar rioting.

But projecting today's figures for demand, supply, and "needs" into the future almost always serves to exaggerate future shortfalls. The reality is that markets always respond. Prices rise to moderate demand and also to stimulate additional supply. Catastrophic doomsday scenarios are easy to predict but rarely materialize. But there is no doubt that water is becoming scarcer in Asia. This will herald many changes but also opportunity as Asia's governments reform, regulate, and invest to avert disaster.

Suggestions for Business Strategists and Scenario Developers

► Billions of dollars in contracts are becoming available around Asia for building and upgrading water distribution and treatment facilities. Many will be available to foreign bidders.

► Water (for both its use and disposal) will become more expensive around Asia as governments reform its pricing to ensure more efficient usage. This will not just affect households but will impact on business and production costs. Heavy water users such as power plants, pulp and paper factories, and mining sites will find themselves under growing pressure to moderate their water usage or at least to pay more. They will also face more media scrutiny and political pressure as they are blamed for water shortages and water price rises.

► Massive reforestation programs in China and India will be implemented to try to halt soil erosion and desertification and to improve water catchment areas.

► Water scarcity alone will see China emerge as one of the world's big grain importers. This alone will exert substantial upwards pressure on international grain prices.

▶ Increasingly, rice will be consumed away from where it is grown. The proportion of rice that is internationally traded is set to rise, with likely commensurate price rises. This will have a significant wealth redistribution impact around Asia: Indonesia and the Philippines will be net losers as they are among the world's big rice importers. But Vietnam, India, and Thailand will gain as they are the world's biggest rice exporters. Rice growers and marketers in the US (currently Arkansas-based Riceland Foods Inc. markets about 25% of the US crop) and Australia can expect significant increases in earnings in future decades.

▶ Resistance to genetically modified rice will lessen as governments strive to improve rice yields. This will be good news for companies such as Monsanto that have invested heavily in this area and to date have faced enormous political flak.

Notes

1 Lees, G., "China faces growing water shortage," WorldPoliticsWatch.com, August 31, 2006.
2 Backman, M., *The Asian Insider: Unconventional Wisdom for Asian Business*, Palgrave Macmillan, 2006, p. 269.
3 Op. cit. Lees, August 31, 2006.
4 *International Herald Tribune*, "China to spend 1 trillion yuan on water," August 23, 2006.
5 *International Herald Tribune*, "From murky waters grow lucrative deals," October 10, 2006.
6 *International Herald Tribune*, "China's water woes imperil grain market," November 11–12, 2006.
7 Bezlova, A., "Tibet: China's little treasure," Asiatimes.com, September 22, 2006.
8 *International Herald Tribune*, "Singapore taps ocean for water and income," September 12, 2006.
9 *Business Times*, "Strong growth seen in China's water sector," June 18, 2007.
10 *International Herald Tribune*, "Water crisis grows worse as India gets richer," September 29, 2006.
11 Energy Information Administration, "Indonesia: Environmental issues," United States, February, 2004.
12 *International Herald Tribune*, "Singapore taps ocean for water and income," September 12, 2006.
13 Op. cit. *International Herald Tribune*, September 29, 2006.
14 Boriss, H., "Commodity profile: Rice," Agricultural Issues Center, University of California, January, 2006.
15 *International Herald Tribune*, "Snap, crackle, boom: rice poised to double," August 15, 2006.
16 *Financial Times*, "Great wall of trees rises to halt the winds of change," March 2, 2005.
17 Op. cit. *International Herald Tribune*, August 15, 2006.
18 Op. cit. Lees, August 31, 2006.
19 *Business Times*, "Bangalore battens down after water ruling," February 6, 2007.

9

China to Have the World's Biggest Number of English Speakers

▷ English proficiency is not as high in India as is commonly believed – 38 million adult Indians are proficient in English. But 56 million adult Filipinos are.

▷ And China is producing 20 million new English speakers *each* year.

▷ China will soon overtake the US as having the biggest number of English speakers.

▷ At the same time, the use of Mandarin in China will rise significantly from half the population today to three-quarters within two or three decades.

Most people assume that English is widely spoken in India. It isn't. Relatively few Indians speak and read it. Most people also assume that among the Asian countries, India has the greatest number of English speakers. It hasn't. And not by a long shot. That honor goes to the Philippines, where 95% of its 90 million-strong population is proficient in English.

Generally, the usual estimate of the proportion of people in India who are competent in English is just 5%. Currently, that's about 38 million people over the age of 15. English has always had an importance in India far beyond the numbers who can actually speak it. A 2005 survey of Indian wage earners found that 16.5% could speak and read English, suggesting that 5% for the total adult population is a reasonable estimate.[1]

History has endowed the populations of Malaysia and Singapore with significant English-language skills. Among many Singaporean and

Malaysian Chinese families particularly, English is not a secondary language but the primary language, the language spoken at home. Many cannot read Chinese at all, speak only a little Chinese and have known only English as their "native" language. And most of the rest of the populations of these two countries have English as a second language. But Malaysia and Singapore are small compared with other Asian countries.

So which Asian country is seizing the lead when it comes to English? It is China: the Chinese are learning English and doing so in their tens of millions.

A corollary of this is that Mandarin usage is increasing in China too. In early 2007, China released the results of a survey of around 500,000 people across 31 provinces and regions. It showed that 53% of those surveyed could speak standard Mandarin – 66% in urban areas but only 45% in rural areas. The rest spoke regional dialects and were unable to communicate effectively in Mandarin. And while only 31% of people aged 60–69 could speak Mandarin, 70% of people aged 15–29 could. This suggests that within two or three decades, around three-quarters of China's population will be able to speak Mandarin, given that it is taught in every school in China.[2]

Good Morning and Welcome to China

Around 7,000 known languages are spoken in the world today. Most are dying out. The top 12 account for more than half the world's population. Mandarin and English are among the top few. An estimated 30 million people are currently studying Mandarin outside China, although the Chinese government expects this to rise to 100 million within several years.[3] But that is nothing like the numbers learning English.

The number of native speakers of English in the world is around 450 million people. Since around 2004, the number of people in the world who speak English as a second language is now more than the number of native speakers, according to a 2006 study for the British Council.

Business process outsourcing (BPO) has been the savior of the Indian economy, the one sector that has allowed India to be seen as cutting edge when a decade ago it was widely assumed to be an economic backwater. And the main characteristic that allowed this sector to take off is the use of English in India. This has not been lost on other countries, particularly China.

But while India continues to produce millions of English speakers, China, almost overnight, has started to produce millions more. But how many millions? At what point can someone be said to speak English?

More people can read it than speak it, which complicates the data. And so it's easier to estimate the numbers learning English than the numbers who can speak it.

China made English compulsory in primary schools from grade 3 in 2001, but in practice the policy has not been implemented evenly, particularly in rural areas. But the government's clear intention is for all young Chinese to learn English and some big cities such as Beijing and Shanghai have introduced English from grade 1.

An estimated 137 million children were enrolled in Chinese primary schools in 2005. The British Council report estimated that the number of children and adults studying English in the formal sector in China in 2005 was an extraordinary 176.7 million.[4]

Additional impetus to learn English has come from the Beijing Olympic Games in 2008 and the 2010 World Expo to be hosted by Shanghai. Beijing has set a goal that by the 2008 Olympics, 80% of all the city's police officers aged under 40 should have at least a reasonable command of English.[5] And retailers, hotels, and restaurants all want their staff to be ready for the influx of English-speaking visitors.

Because of these initiatives, China now produces more than 20 million English-language speakers each year. This means that China will soon have more people proficient in English than India, if that is not the case already. Soon, it will even pass the US as the country with the world's biggest pool of English speakers.

China's push for English proficiency means that more non-native English speakers are currently learning English than ever before in history. The demand for English-language teachers and resources such as textbooks has become enormous.

China is believed to recruit around 100,000 foreigners each year to come to China to teach English, and at any one time there are something like 150,000 foreign English teachers in China. The central government does not appear to have an explicit policy on foreign English teachers. Instead, the situation has simply evolved. The basic requirements tend to be that teachers should have a BA, be from a country where English is the first language, and have some sort of English-language teaching qualification, such as a Teaching English as a Foreign Language (TEFL) certificate.

Perhaps because of China's lead, other Asian countries have decided to devote more resources to upgrade and extend their English-language proficiency. Thailand, the Philippines, and Taiwan are examples. More English is taught in Thai schools, for example, than ever before. And Malaysia made English (and not Malay, the national language) a basic requirement for all foreign workers in 2003.[6]

English is not only useful for trade, business, and tourism but at the individual level is regarded as the gateway to work opportunities in the world's rich countries. The globalization of the world's major universities has also contributed to the greater desirability of English. The main language of instruction in most of Europe's top management schools is English. And universities compete against each other on a global level for students, now that English has become the main language of instruction among the top universities. In 2003–04, around 1,500 Masters programs were offered in English at universities in countries where English is not the first language.[7] University academics too have become one global labor pool among which English proficiency provides access to the greatest range of opportunities.

What will this all mean? Certainly a shared language reduces transaction costs. It allows markets to function more efficiently and transparently. And it increases the mobility of labor. But the implications of so many mainland Chinese learning English are huge, for China and the rest of the world. India, already facing skilled labor shortages and rising costs in its BPO sector, will see its competitiveness dramatically eroded. Chinese companies will be better able to market their products compared with the clumsy brochures and web marketing currently employed. And the pace of technology transfer will quicken as more and more Chinese can read the latest technology and academic journals in English and keep up with the latest technological developments.

Suggestions for Business Strategists and Scenario Developers

► With so many in China learning English, Mandarin-speaking skills are not going to be as necessary as many forecasts predict.

► China will emerge as an important center for BPO, taking business away from India.

► China will emerge as a new and rapidly growing market for English-language magazines, films, books, and other media.

► China's competitors in Asia will also lift their focus on English-language education to better compete with China. Already, English is the preferred second language in Vietnam instead of French, for example. The region-wide demand for teachers of English and English teaching tools will continue.

Notes

1   As cited in Graddol, D., *English Next*, The British Council, 2006, p. 94.
2   Xinhua report, March 7, 2007.
3   Op. cit. Graddol, 2006, p. 63.
4   Op. cit. Graddol, 2006, p. 95.
5   Op. cit. Graddol, 2006, p. 95.
6   Op. cit. Graddol, 2006, p. 38.
7   Op. cit. Graddol, 2006, p. 74.

10 China's HR Nightmare

▷ China will have 25 million tertiary students in 2010. But quantity is not the issue. It's quality.

▷ China will need 75,000 top-level executives with global experience by 2010, according to one estimate. In 2005, it was thought to have just 5,000.

▷ More than 100,000 of China's brightest go overseas to study each year. Most don't come back.

China has plenty of workers. But few are management material. Fewer still are creative, lateral thinkers. This is no small matter. It is probably the most important supply-side constraint that threatens China's great march to sustained prosperity.

China is committed to upgrading its universities. But there are two problems. The state university sector can barely keep up with demand. And the types of courses emphasized tend to be the sciences and technology.

China claims to have 3 million university students but that's out of a population of 1.3 billion people.[1] On the other hand, the US has 17 million out of a population of 300 million. Defining what is meant by "university" in China is problematic, which alone leads to a variety of estimates as to how many university graduates China actually produces.

The government now spends more on education than ever before. But that spending has barely kept pace with economic growth, so as a proportion of the economy, education spending has been almost static. A 1993 target of spending 4% of GDP on education by 2000 went unmet, so the goalposts were shifted. It is now hoped that the 4% figure will be met in 2010.[2]

A 1986 requirement on local government that all children must receive at least nine years education was not met with an adequate funding increase and so China has not yet met this target either. Nor have funding increases been adequate to meet the more than threefold increase in the number of tertiary students since 1999. The problem will only grow. There are around 15 million tertiary students today. By 2010 there will be around 25 million.

Quantity is one problem but so too is quality. The liberal arts, which require critical thinking about politics, economics, and society, present too much of a challenge for China's government. And so it has placed little or no emphasis on these areas. In 2004, for example, only 16% of China's university population was enrolled in arts and humanities and of that almost half were enrolled in languages.[3] But creativity and questioning minds is what China most lacks among its graduates and what multinational companies most complain about when it comes to the quality of their new employees.

The importance of liberal arts also includes the ability to think "laterally." One educator who has worked in China and Singapore says:

> I find that most students in Asia that have attended local schools have a very low tolerance for ambiguity. In case discussions, it is the rare student who takes a truly bold stand and/or leap of faith when solving a company's problems. Most prefer the comfort of saying "there's not enough data or information to make an informed decision" … While Asian managers are highly regarded implementers, far fewer are innovative strategists. It is the difference between extrapolating trends and deriving meaning that leads to true value from the trend's implications. Sadly, most Asian managers fall into the former category.

Instead of emphasizing courses that teach lateral thinking, China has poured money into creating world-class university laboratories, for example, and attracting top-level science and technology academic staff from abroad. This is all very worthy but it is still only half of what is required to provide a full university curriculum in a Western sense. Lin Jianhua, the executive vice-president of Peking University, has said:[4]

> Right now, I don't think any university in China has an atmosphere comparable to the older Western universities – Harvard or Oxford – in terms of freedom of expression.

But even when it comes to sciences and technology, very few universities in China are comparable in quality to universities in Europe or the US. There are a handful of top institutions and then there are the rest and the gap between them can be large. This gap means that raw numbers are misleading. Gary Gereffi and Vivek Wadha at Duke University were intrigued by the commonly repeated assertion that only 70,000 engineers graduate from US universities each year but that China produced 600,000 engineering graduates and India 350,000.[5] When they took a closer look at the numbers and compared like with like, they found that the numbers of graduates from rigorous four-year engineering degree programs rose to 137,000 for the US but fell to 112,000 in respect of India and 351,000 for China. The Chinese figures probably still exaggerate its standing because a large number are not engineering graduates as would be commonly understood in the West but more the caliber of car mechanics.

In another study, McKinsey Global Institute conducted interviews with 83 HR professionals involved with hiring local graduates in low-wage countries and found that between 2003 and 2008, China would produce 15.7 million graduates, from which only 1.2 million, or less than 10%, would be suitable for a multinational employer in the nine occupations studied: engineers, life science researchers, finance workers, accountants, generalists, quantitative analysts, doctors, nurses, and support staff.

China's government intrudes in research like nowhere else. Not a single university in China has the freedom of expression and inquiry that is routine among top universities in the US, the UK, or Australia. Often the intrusion is unnecessary. Academics self-censor. They know the questions they shouldn't ask, the phrases they should use, the no-go areas. Students are watched by government and Communist Party agents. The Internet is monitored. Type certain "sensitive" words into a search engine at some campus computers and access to that search engine can be automatically shut down across the campus.

Free inquiry is not encouraged and so the sciences are deemed "safer." But even then, China might produce many good engineering graduates, for example, but almost no great ones. It's one of the reasons why not a single Nobel Prize in any discipline has ever been awarded to China. But then these criticisms are true of higher education around much of Asia. Students are turned out who are good at following orders rather than being creative. They are competent rather than clever.

Business schools have similar problems.[6] The Ministry of Education (MOE) first licensed schools to grant MBAs in 1991, beginning with 9 universities with 100 students. By 2001 the MOE had approved 62 institutions with 10,000 students enrolled. But after the top group of about 13 schools come a stream of inferior institutions offering low-quality MBA programs, taught in Mandarin by poorly trained faculties. Not surprisingly, they churn out graduates with few discernible skills. Others are little more than "diploma mills" that provide credentials for a fee but precious little education. All this, when McKinsey has estimated that China will require 75,000 top-level executives with global experience by 2010 – about 70,000 more than the current number.[7]

Many Chinese universities formed partnerships with US, Australian, European, and Hong Kong schools to offer better quality state-approved MBA programs. The elite Chinese universities, such as Peking and Tsinghua University in Beijing and Fudan University in Shanghai, have both forged strong links with top US schools. MIT has an MBA program at Tsinghua and many of its faculty have each spent six months at the Sloan school. Others have spent time at Harvard. Fudan has been sending faculty to MIT for the past 10 years. Also, some multinational companies have become big donors to Chinese schools: ABN-Amro, Bayer, Citigroup, Alcatel, and Philips among them. This helps to improve the education that can be offered and it gives the companies an option to be the first to review the best of the new graduates.

Through these partnerships, the Chinese aim to create a superleague of universities that can produce graduates of the right caliber. But even these top graduates often lack adequate English skills and problem-solving abilities. The problem is linked to the poor system of elementary and secondary education. The universities can only work with what they're given. But it's also linked to how the universities themselves teach and how they assess students, which is heavily focused on individuals' examination results.

The problem of there being too few good graduates in China is exacerbated by the massive outflow from China of promising students to attend universities abroad, who then stay there. Research by the Chinese Academy of Social Sciences suggests that of the approximately one million young Chinese who have studied abroad since the 1980s, around two-thirds chose to stay overseas after graduation. Since 2002, more than 100,000 students have gone abroad to study each year but the number of returnees hovers between 20,000 and 30,000.[8]

Another problem is that many institutions attempt to pass themselves off as high caliber when they are not. Others are downright fraudulent and offer fake qualifications or they themselves are fake. One example emerged in late 2006: the Sino-European International Management Institute (SEIMI), which claimed on its website to be based in both Beijing and Fontainebleau, outside Paris. The French address happened to be that for INSEAD, Europe's top business school. SEIMI's website provided names and photographs of faculty staff, most of whom are France-based INSEAD lecturers and professors. The problem with all of this is that the SEIMI had nothing to do with INSEAD, or any of its staff.

In its Chinese-English, the website said:

> SEIMI has been recognized internationally nowadays. The institute is one of the pioneers in providing one-year MBA courses. It now has more than 3,000 students applying for MBA program and 400 on-job doctorates.

This is all true of INSEAD. But it was not true of SEIMI, which, ironically, listed intellectual property law as a component topic of one of its postgraduate programs. The Institute did not offer classes but merely assessment via the Internet. It is not clear whether China includes "graduates" from such institutions in its annual totals or not.

Education in China badly needs a shake-up more than it needs new resources. How students are taught is what needs to change, rather than pushing through ever increasing numbers of students just so they can possess questionable credentials. But how soon is that going to happen? Not any time soon. Some of the problems are ingrained – they are cultural – and will take generations to remedy. Others relate to the desire of China's leaders to maintain their power and the power of the Party at any cost. And China's leaders will sacrifice propriety long before they ever sacrifice their power.

Suggestions for Business Strategists and Scenario Developers

▶ There is no shortage of graduates in China. But getting good local staff with leadership and management potential is extremely difficult. The dearth of such talent means that many Chinese are promoted too early. Many also have inflated perceptions of their abilities. All of this helps to limit the growth of many enterprises in China, irrespective of the demand they face. Companies' strategies need to take a realistic view of the talent shortages they will face in China and allocate sufficient resources to internal staff development.

▶ Recruitment costs in China are also high. The truthfulness of résumés needs to be assessed. Academic transcripts and qualifications are often fake or embellished. Also, many higher education institutions have grand names but are either bogus or are principally fee generating, handing out low-quality qualifications.

▶ To generalize: Chinese graduates are good at following instructions and are hardworking. They are not good at teamwork, sharing information with colleagues, dealing with ambiguity, and undertaking tasks that call for creativity. Managers in China need to allow for this and to implement training programs that foster teamwork and creativity. It's an enormous task that requires expatriate managers to be patient and nurturing, and have strong mentoring skills. Individuals who do not have these skills should reconsider taking an assignment in China.

Notes

1 Chee, H. and West, C., *Myths about Doing Business in China*, Palgrave Macmillan, 2004, p. 110.
2 See *The Economist*, "Chaos in the classroom," August 12, 2006.
3 From a presentation by the Corporate Leadership Council in association with Universum, "Winning the graduate recruiting battle in China," September/October, 2006.
4 *International Herald Tribune*, "China strives for world-class universities," October 28, 2005.
5 As cited in Tripathi, S., "India's skill shortage," *Wall Street Journal Asia*, January 5, 2006.
6 For more on this, see Backman, M. and Butler, C., *Big in Asia: 30 Strategies for Business Success*, Palgrave Macmillan, 2007.
7 Lavelle, L., "China's B-school boom," *Business Week*, January 9, 2006.
8 As cited in *Business Times*, "China suffers from worst brain drain in the world," February 14, 2007.

India's HR Nightmare

▷ India underspends on education like it underspends on infrastructure.

▷ India has its much celebrated Indian Institutes of Technology that turn out high-class graduates. The only problem is that they enroll just 4,000 new students each year, and this for a country with a billion-plus population.

▷ India has too few good business schools. It's almost fifty times easier to gain admission to Stanford's business school program than it is to get into the IIM Ahmedabad business school.

What is most likely to ruin India's prospects for continued economic growth? Its famously atrocious road network? The corrupt and inefficient ports? Relentless red tape? War with Pakistan? Probably none of these. Ironically for a country with a billion-plus population, it is more likely to be a lack of manpower and, more specifically, a lack of management and leadership skills.

Around 60% of India's population is aged under 25 so education issues are paramount. But according to a paper released by India's Commerce Ministry, at 11% of the relevant age group, enrollment in higher education in India is low compared with comparable economies. For example, enrolment in China is at 13% but in the Philippines it's at 31%, in Thailand it's 19%, and in Malaysia it's 27%.

Not only that, but, according to the paper, at US$406, India also has one of the lowest public expenditures on higher education per student. This compares with US$625 for Malaysia, US$666 for Indonesia, US$2,728 for China, and US$3,986 in Brazil.[1]

It's not all bad. At the apex of India's education pyramid are seven Indian Institutes of Technology (IITs). Set up in the 1950s by the country's first Prime Minister Jawaharlal Nehru, they turn out world-class graduates. But even today, enrollment in the IITs is limited to around 4,000 places at the first degree level and even fewer at the postgraduate level. These numbers are infinitesimal, given India's population. What of the other 11 million or so students in India's approximately 18,000 other colleges and universities?[2] The reality is that they face substantially inferior training that is heavy on passive note taking and light on opportunities for teamwork, creativity, debate, and discussion. Their English skills are often poorly developed – for example teachers often use bad grammar and have heavily accented English. Nor are their writing skills and anything else that might be marketable developed to a high level. And the tragedy is that many of those in this second tier of education are capable of undertaking the work at the IITs and miss out simply because so few places are on offer. This two-tier system almost deliberately locks millions of Indian students into an inferior education system so that the seven IITs can look good.

A consequence of this pinprick of excellence in a sea of dross is that the vast majority of Indian graduates are unemployable as graduates. One study estimated that just 10% of Indian graduates with generalist degrees, 15% of finance and accounting graduates, and 25% of engineering graduates were considered employable by multinational companies.[3]

It's almost a similar story when it comes to business schools. There are a handful of excellent schools and then there are the rest. The Indian Institutes of Management (IIMs) have the toughest admission standards in the world. The IIM Ahmedabad admits approximately 250 out of 140,000 applicants for its Postgraduate Program of Management – that's almost 1 in 600.[4] This compares with the acceptance rate at the Stanford Graduate School of Business of around 1 in 13. But with such stringent entrance standards, do the IIMs actually teach students significant new skills, or do they simply operate as a screening mechanism for employers who clamor after IIM graduates, knowing that simply by having been admitted to an IIM they are the very best that India has to offer by way of management talent? Almost certainly, it is more the latter than the former, particularly as the IIMs use little more than the standard texts used in, say, US business schools. Nor do their teaching methods vary much either.

While it is true that more privately funded engineering and business colleges are springing up across India, they are of variable quality and invariably homegrown. What India desperately needs in its higher education system is more competition, new ideas, and more funding. The obvious solution is to allow excellent foreign institutions to set up campuses in India, names such as Harvard, Yale, Princeton, Cambridge, and Oxford. But as is usual in India, the government has agreed to this but with so many caveats that in practice it is a no. For example, it wants to regulate the fees that foreign institutions can charge such that none of them would find it commercially feasible to set up in India.

The issue descended into infighting between the Commerce Ministry, which wanted foreign universities to have greater access, and the Human Resources Development Ministry, which argues against this for vague "national interest" reasons. The more likely reason is to protect the IITs from competition. The starting pay for an IIT professor is less than many call center workers can now earn in India. Local campuses of the likes of Harvard and Cambridge would strip the IITs of many of their younger and more dynamic teaching staff.

What this all means is that the middle and upper echelons of Indian business are severely starved of leadership talent. And now that India's economy has started to grow rapidly, this means that many young graduates are promoted more rapidly than their skills development ordinarily would allow for. It means that 25-year-olds, for example, are expected to handle the responsibilities of a seasoned 40-year-old, which few can successfully do.

One way around the problem is for employers to take graduates who show promise and then educate them in-house. Software firms tend to scoop up all the best graduates after carefully screening them and then put them through their own in-house induction programs to give them basic training. But it's an expensive process, and costs as much as US$4,250 per entry-level engineer.[5] Infosys, one of India's largest IT companies, spends well over US$100 million a year now on training its staff.[6]

Rent Seeking Costs

India and Indians are justifiably proud of the IITs. Sometimes they go overboard in their enthusiasm. In a speech in 2006, the IMF's chief economist Raghuram Rajan said: "How many advanced countries even now can boast of schools of the caliber of the IITs?"[7] The answer is quite a few. Not only that, but the success of the higher education systems of most developed countries relates to how many world-class graduates they produce. But for India, the number of world-class graduates produced on a per capita basis is appalling. The IITs are excellent but there are too few of them, meaning that too many adequate candidates are forced to chase an artificially low number of places. Quite possibly, the quality of the output of the IITs (and the IIMs) has less to do with what goes on in them and more to do with the quality of the inputs. Universities everywhere will produce stunning graduates if they let almost no one in. But that should not be the goal of a publicly funded higher education system. The goal should be to educate people – the more the better.

Getting into an IIT is so coveted that high-paid coaches have set up in business to help prepare candidates for the IIT entrance exams. In turn, places on their courses are coveted. It's easier to get into Harvard than it is to even get a spot in some of these coaching clinics, much less an IIT itself. One, an academy in Hyderabad cited in the media in 2006, claimed to accept 146 students out of 10,000 applicants. The 15-year-olds are then coached for two years just so they can have a better chance at passing an IIT exam.[8]

Expenditure on this sort of preparation for the IIT exams has been estimated at around US$680 million annually – quite apart from the opportunity costs of all the swotting of teenage Indians aimed not at learning so much as passing exams for courses that the vast majority will not be accepted for. Many students even begin coaching at the age of 12 – five years prior to taking the IIT exams.

This sort of expense is analogous to the expenditure by business on courting politicians so that they might be awarded special privileges such as permits and licenses that will help them generate above-average economic returns. It amounts to directly unproductive expenditure and as such represents a dead weight cost to the economy.

So India's system of elite IITs and IIMs means that it loses on two counts. Far too few graduates are produced and too much cost is involved in attempting to secure scarce places. Universities should be about education and not winning a lottery. Meanwhile, generations of good Indians must accept substandard higher education, while a lucky few are able to study at an IIT. It's one reason why India's better known companies now choose to invest billions abroad where capable managers are more easily found (see Chapter 6).

Suggestions for Business Strategists and Scenario Developers

► Hiring the best local managers in India is phenomenally expensive. There are just too few relative to demand. Nor is the Indian government taking steps to alleviate the process. In fact, by curtailing the setting up of foreign-owned and managed graduate schools in India, the government is helping to worsen the problem relative to demand. Many companies find that they need to grow their own managers. It is an expensive process. Scenario planning and growth strategies need to take a realistic account of the difficulties in finding the right local senior staff in India.

▶ English-language capabilities are not as strong in India as is widely assumed. The majority of Indians do not speak English, and relatively few, given the size of the population, have adequate written English.

Notes

1   The paper is titled, "Higher education in India and General Agreement on Trade and Services (GATS): An opportunity," (September, 2006), and is cited in *Asia Times*, "India's million-dollar education question," September, 2006.
2   *International Herald Tribune*, "Elitist college system stymies India," November 27, 2006.
3   Op. cit. *Asia Times*, September, 2006.
4   *International Herald Tribune*, "From India business schools to top of world's boardrooms," August 24, 2006.
5   *International Herald Tribune*, "For growing firms, a mismatch of skills," January 27, 2006.
6   *The Economist*, "The search for talent," October 7, 2006.
7   *Business Times*, "Why India needs Harvard and Stanford," February 1, 2006.
8   Ibid.

Wanted! 250 Million Wives: Asia's Shocking Gender Imbalance

12

> ▷ India and China will have 250 million more men than women in 2030.
> ▷ Around half will be prime age males unable to find a wife.
> ▷ For every 1,000 boys born in India and China, 100 fewer girls are born.

Why do parents in Asia prefer sons? The reasons are many: sons carry on the family name, they inherit property in most of Asia's cultures, they are a means of income support in old age, and in India the high cost of providing a dowry means that daughters can represent a huge financial cost for little return. Also in India, Hindu custom dictates that it is the sons who must perform the cremation rights. No sons and the rites are incomplete. In China, Korea, and even Japan, not having sons to carry on the family name is to dishonor the ancestors.

For centuries in Asia, baby daughters all too often were suffocated shortly after birth. But since the 1980s, when ultrasound machines became available that allowed parents to know the sex of their unborn children, the process has been brought forward. Abortion has become the substitute for infanticide. But more so. So much so in fact that many parts of Asia will shortly face gender imbalances more serious than have ever been faced anywhere in history. Indeed, by 2030, if current trends continue, India and China alone will have around 250 million men more than women, many of whom will be "surplus" males – males unable to marry because of a shortage of women.

This is in cultures that place great importance on marriage. And that is the irony: cultures so hell-bent on having sons that millions of men will be unable to marry and thus have the sons that are so coveted.

So in which Asian countries is the gender imbalance the most serious? South Korea, Pakistan, Bangladesh, Nepal, India, and China all face this problem. But the problem is most acute in India and China. It has been serious in Korea, where for every 1,000 girls born, there are 1,108 boys. Several years ago the figure was 1,013 boys for every 1,000 girls. The decline in the imbalance has been due to government education programs and better enforcement of laws against sex-selection abortion. But the problem is still serious enough that many young Korean men today must look abroad for a wife.

Marriage brokers offer to find wives for Korean men in Vietnam, for example. Ethnic Koreans who live in China are another source. Women also come from Mongolia, the Philippines, Thailand, Cambodia, and Uzbekistan. In 2005, marriages to foreigners accounted for an extraordinary 14% of all marriages in South Korea, up from 4% in 2000.[1] Billboards advertising the services of companies that help to arrange marriages to foreigners have sprung up across South Korea. The Korean Consumer Protection Board estimates that there are now between 2,000 and 3,000 such agencies.

The Extent of the Problem

It's not fashionable to praise British colonialism for anything. But in fact, the British colonial administration in India, as in most other British colonies, did much to combat appallingly unfair local customs that were aimed squarely at keeping women subjugated.

Concubinage was outlawed in Hong Kong, for example. And in India, the age of consent was raised in 1891 so that it was illegal to force child brides as young as 10 to have sexual intercourse with elderly husbands. Sati, the custom whereby widows leaped to their deaths into the flames of their husband's funeral pyre, was outlawed in 1829. And in 1856, the Hindu Widow Remarriage Act was passed, giving Hindu women who had been widowed the right to remarry. Custom had dictated that they could not. It was not customary for the dead husband's family to look after them either, which means that many were forced into begging and prostitution.[2] Despite the law, this tradition continues.

Across India, daughters still represent a liability for many families. They will eventually belong to their future husband's family, so any expenditure on their health or education represents expenditure that will end up benefiting others. The problem is compounded by dowry payments, which, although illegal, continue to be demanded in some communities.

In developed countries, the natural sex ratio slightly favors boys at birth. But in India, the ratio of girls to boys born has been steadily falling. In 1961, 976 girls were born for each 1,000 boys. By 2002, the figure for girls had declined to 927. By 2005, the estimate was 896.[3] There are some regions now that have as few as 6 girls for every 10 boys. This has contributed to a terrible imbalance overall. By 2002, India had around 35 million more men than women. By 2006, the figure was closer to 65 million. This is the extreme opposite of the case in developed economies, where, because women tend to live longer than men, there are more women overall. The US, for example, with a population of 300 million, had 9 million more women than men in 2006.

The effect of the low birth-rate of girls in India is exacerbated by the treatment that many girl babies encounter. Infanticide remains a risk but that still doesn't tell the whole story. Simple neglect accounts for many deaths: sons are looked after better than girls. A son will have more spent on his healthcare should he become sick, for example. He will be taken to hospital sooner and have more medicines bought for him. It's simply a matter of economics: sons have a higher net present value than daughters. And so at present, around a million more girls than boys die during the first five years of life, for each wave of cohorts.[4] Girls are also less likely to be sent to school, which means that they are less likely to find good employment to break the cycle of poverty.

A 2006 study by a professor at the University of Toronto and a medical researcher based in India published in *The Lancet*, a British medical journal, estimated that each year, around 500,000 fewer female babies are born in India than should be the case, allowing the researchers to estimate that from 1985 to 2005 as many as 10 million female fetuses might have been aborted. This coincides with the increased availability of ultrasound equipment that allows the sex of an unborn child to be determined. The researchers found that among the 133,738 births they surveyed, in families where the first child was a girl, the ratio of girls to boys among second children was 759 girls per 1,000 boys. And if there were two daughters, then the ratio was 719 for every 1,000 boys, suggesting that many families took steps to ensure that at least one of their children was male.[5]

A ban was introduced in 1994 to prevent doctors from revealing the sex of an unborn child to the parents as a way of combating this problem. A pregnant woman seeking sex-selection services faces a fine of 50,000 rupees (about US$1,100) and doctors found to be assisting could have their medical licenses suspended. But the law often is ignored and it's badly enforced.

The Lancet study found that the gender imbalance among children actually increased among better educated and better off families, suggesting that they were better at finding ways to get around the law. They could afford the procedures to determine their unborn child's sex and then the procedures to do something about it.

As ultrasound equipment becomes cheaper, more Indian clinics will be able to acquire it, particularly in poorer and more remote areas, and so the gender imbalance will worsen.

In China, the one-child policy has encouraged similar abortion practices. Many families feel that if they're allowed only one child, then it had better be a boy. With fewer children, all the reasons for wanting a son are magnified. By 2006, it was estimated that China had 40 million bachelors due to the sex ratio imbalance. And overall, out of a population of 1,314 million, there were almost 80 million more men than women. But the situation may not be exactly as in India.

As always, things are not so clear-cut. Families in many parts of Asia do prefer sons over daughters and do take steps to ensure that they have sons rather than daughters. But the degree to which selective abortion and infanticide are responsible for the huge imbalances that we now see is likely to have been exaggerated. Pregnant women with hepatitis B have been shown to be far more likely give birth to boys than girls. A 2005 Harvard University study took this finding and applied it to birth-rates in several countries that have a substantial gender imbalance, including China and India, where, as it happens, hepatitis B is prevalent. It was found that the virus could explain 75% of the missing female births in China and 20% of the missing female births in India.[6] This suggests that although sex-selection abortion is a significant contributor to the problem in China, an important remedy will be the eradication of hepatitis B. This will be less effective in India though as a means of remedying the gender imbalance.

Social Destabilization

It has been estimated that by 2020, India will have 28 million more men aged 15–34 than similarly aged women. In China, the figure will be around 30 million and in Pakistan it will be 3–5 million.[7] And assuming that both China and India will have populations of 1.6 billion in 2030 and an average ratio of men to women of 1.08 (less than at present), then in 2030, both will have more than 250 million men more than women.

It's difficult to quantify the social impact that such extreme gender imbalances will have. All we can do is guess what might happen. Unfortunately, there is little to say that's positive.

Better educated men, those from wealthier backgrounds, or those with better earning prospects overall tend to be the ones who find a wife. This means that surplus males, those males in China and India who do not find a wife because there are too few to go around, tend to be less well educated and from poorer backgrounds. In China, for example, 94% of all unmarried people between the ages of 28 and 49 are male and 97% of them have not completed high school.[8]

But high value is put on marriage in these societies, and certainly high value is put on having sons. Their inability to marry and have children will see many marginalized in society. Inevitably, this will lead to a greater tendency to violence and criminality, which will threaten social stability and security. There's much to be said for the moderating influence of a wife, a family, and all the obligations and responsibilities that go with it.

In China, men who do not raise families of their own are known as *guang gun-er* or "bare branches" on the family tree. They tend to join the floating population and congregate in cities, where without the stability and responsibility of family life, they are more likely to be involved in crime.[9]

In India, particularly in the larger, poorer, more rural states, some researchers do not think that fewer women relative to men will raise women's value in the eyes of men. Instead, they think that there will be increased crime and violence, more trafficking in women and underage girls, and more prostitution. Already women are being trafficked from poorer neighboring countries such as Bangladesh and Nepal to be married off in India, but also from poorer regions within India.

Says one field researcher: "I ask you, could you send your young daughter out onto the street happily if there were nothing but young men around?"[10] Polyandrous unions will become more common, whereby one woman is shared between several brothers. But rather than being coveted, such women will have low social status in the family and in society more broadly. Putting it crudely, communal assets are always valued less than those that are privately held.

There are signs that in some parts of India at least there is a reversal of the dowry tradition, so that families of young men are now willing to pay a high "groom" price (instead of there being a bride price) to the parents of daughters so that their sons can have a wife. Might this lead to a greater appreciation of the value of women? In some cases, yes, and quite literally so. The more costly an asset, the greater the incentive to look after it. But then it will also make it more difficult for women to leave an unhappy marriage. After all, no one wants to see an expensive asset walk out the door.

Another implication of the male–female imbalance relates to population ageing. China is one of Asia's most rapidly ageing countries – its elderly already number more than the entire populations of many industrial countries. One issue with China's growing lack of females compared with males is that traditional caregivers – women and more particularly wives – will be in short supply to take care of China's elderly. Traditionally, the elderly are looked after in the home. But with traditional caregivers in short supply, the shift toward retirement homes and aged care accommodation will be hastened.

Export Men: One Way to Mop Up

China has been criticized when it funds infrastructure projects in Africa, for example, for insisting that it bring its own workers from China to do work that could easily have been performed by local workers. In Pakistan, China funded the construction of a port in the coastal city of Gwadar that ultimately will be used to ship Central Asian oil and gas to China. It was inaugurated in 2007. Five hundred Chinese laborers worked on-site at the peak of the construction in 2002.[11] Again, the workers could have been sourced locally, but China insisted that they come from China.

This is one way in which China can alleviate the problem of surplus males – by exporting them. Certainly hundreds of thousands of mostly young Chinese men have migrated both legally and illegally from China in recent years and flooded Africa. They have also become more apparent in Europe too, doing low-paid work or selling pirated DVDs in many of Europe's cities.

Another way in which surplus males can be occupied is to expand armies. It's the age-old solution everywhere – if you have lots of poorly educated, potentially troublesome young men, then pack them off into military service. China has been reducing the size of its army but it might need to halt further reduction simply to "mop up" single young men. And again, they can be sent overseas, particularly now that China has shown more interest in contributing troops to international peacekeeping forces, but also if China increasingly wishes to use its own troops to protect its investments abroad as it has done in Sudan, for example.

Suggestions for Business Strategists and Scenario Developers

► Expanding armies to mop up surplus males will see greater demand for military clothing, ration packs, and military housing – all requirements that in Asia are increasingly contracted out to the private sector.

► Huge gender imbalances among young adults will see a strong desire among many young Indian and Chinese men to migrate. This will mean that even more will be prepared to work as expatriates, with the additional desire for them to leave India and China so that they might find a wife. This will help to keep down the costs of attracting and hiring them as employees.

► Niche introduction agencies that seek to match Indian and Chinese men with Chinese and Indian females from the diaspora communities will thrive, as will Internet matchmaking sites that seek to introduce couples from different locations. Already, there are many Indian sites in which single young men and women list all the usual data but also their caste.

► The Hindu tradition that discourages widows from remarrying will break down in India, thus alleviating a large social problem in a country where sadly it remains a fact that most women are only a husband away from abject poverty.

Notes

1 *International Herald Tribune*, "Also globalized: Asia's marriage market," February 22, 2007.
2 *London Review of Books*, "Calcutta in the Cotswolds," March 3, 2005.
3 Leidl, P., "The promise of equality: Gender equity, reproductive health and the Millennium Development Goals," in *The State of World Population 2005*, The United Nations Population Fund, 2006.
4 *International Herald Tribune*, "The dangers of Asia's preference for sons," May 13, 2004.
5 *International Herald Tribune*, "India's lost daughters: Abortion toll in millions," January 10, 2006.
6 Cited in Tripathi, S., "Unsuitable girls," *Guardian*, January 11, 2006.
7 Op. cit. *International Herald Tribune*, May 13, 2004.
8 Canadian Broadcasting Corporations News, "Gender imbalance 'threatens social stability,'" August 29, 2006.
9 Op. cit. *International Herald Tribune*, May 13, 2004.
10 Op. cit. Leidl, P., 2006.
11 *International Herald Tribune*, "China builds a port in Pakistan," September 9, 2004.

13

Asia's Meaningless Borders

▷ Asia is home to millions of illegal migrants from other Asian countries. Millions more work legally in neighboring countries. Consider this along with smuggling, and Asia's countries are losing their definition; their borders are increasingly meaningless. Add in billions of dollars in foreign investment and most Asian governments' appeals to nationalism are undermined. What does it mean to be a proud Malaysian or Singaporean, for example? Increasingly little.

What good are Asia's borders? Many are not much good at all. Tourists, expatriates, and business travelers tend to observe them, but in many instances the locals don't, either for trade or immigration. Add to that legal migration and Asia's nation-states are becoming increasingly meaningless. Asian governments can sign all the regional economic integration agreements they like but for the most part this is not driving Asia forwards. It is simply catching up with reality. And in decades to come, Asia's borders and its governments will be even more meaningless, as goods, services, and people circulate to wherever the opportunities are, regardless of the preferences of the region's governments.

Smuggling: The Real Free Trade

Smuggling is so rife in some Asian countries that their trade statistics hold little meaning. This is particularly so for Burma, Laos, Cambodia,

Thailand, and Indonesia. But aren't there now more free-trade agreements and the like that render smuggling if not unnecessary then at least not so profitable? Yes, but that is partly the problem. There are now 109 free-trade agreements in East Asia and 192 for the Asia Pacific region as a whole.[1] Each requires documentation and certification. Some importers actually prefer to pay tariffs than comply with all the paperwork needed to ensure duty-free trade. The other option is to bypass the process altogether by smuggling.

Singapore does not publish its data on trade between it and Indonesia. The reason is because Singapore's figures bear little relationship to the numbers compiled by the Indonesian government. In 2002, for example, it is known that Singapore recorded non-oil exports to Indonesia of US$5.25 billion. Indonesia's Central Bureau of Statistics (BPS) reported imports from Singapore of just US$2.44 billion. Singapore put its non-oil imports from Indonesia at US$7.41 billion. And the BPS put the figure at US$4.6 billion.[2] Indonesia's other trading partners record very different trade statistics with Indonesia compared with the Indonesian figures too. The biggest data gaps relate to Indonesia's trade with Singapore, China, Germany, Japan, Malaysia, and the US.[3] Some of the difference is due to statistical error. Most though is due to smuggling, which runs to many billions of dollars each year.

Private individuals are involved but so too are various provincial governments and the country's navy and police. Sometimes, the smuggling operations of the various arms of government in Indonesia cut across each other. For example, it was reported in mid-2004 that the Indonesian navy had impounded a boat carrying more than 1,000 cubic meters of undocumented logs off the east coast of Sumatra. It was later determined that the boat was linked to Indonesia's police force.[4]

Malaysia also has a smuggling problem. Both Malaysia and Indonesia subsidize the price that consumers pay for gasoline and so smugglers make arbitrage profits by buying gasoline in these countries to sell elsewhere. Indonesia estimated that it lost US$862 million in 2005 by subsidizing fuel that was then smuggled out of the country. Malaysia estimated that it lost US$175 million.[5]

Economic Migrants

But the real impact of Asia's porous borders relates to people. Ethnic groups have long drifted around Asia. Southeast Asia particularly has been a giant, borderless melting pot for centuries. Various kingdoms unified much of the region at various times too. For example, the Majapahit Empire, based in Eastern Java in the fourteenth century, also had states in the Malay Peninsular, Sumatra, and Borneo under its influence.

And so, historically, Asia and particularly Southeast Asia were not a series of discrete bundles of nationalities and ethnicities neatly separated by well-defined borders as suggested by arrangements today. The South China Sea was the Mediterranean of the East: trade and migration flourished in every direction. Émigré merchant communities sprung up around the region. Muslim traders were everywhere and so too were Chinese traders. People mixed and cultures blended. Traditional children's stories in Islamic Brunei are full of tales of Chinese dragons, for example. Kashmiri silver and goldwork ended up as part of the Dalai Lama's regalia in Tibet. And Persian loan-words entered the Thai language. The Persian for "grape," for example, is pronounced *anguur*. In Thai, it's *angun*.

But it wasn't just trade that led to such cultural cross-pollination. Whole communities resettled across borders. The Thai silk industry was founded on the back of the cottage silk weaving of the Muslim Cham people, who had settled in Bangkok but have their ancestral roots in southern Vietnam.

Modern Malaysia comprises an astonishing pastiche of ethnicities, relatively few of which can claim to have ancestral origins in what comprises Malaysia today. The immigration of most of Malaysia's Chinese and Indians was facilitated by the British but the Malays too largely come from somewhere else, particularly from Sumatra in Indonesia. And the Penang Malays (known locally as the *Pinang Mamak*) are among the most exotic, being a mixture of Malay, Javanese, Sumatran, Turkish, Indian, and Arab stock, reflecting Penang's position on trade routes and as one of the collection points in Southeast Asia for pilgrims on the journey to Mecca.

Many of the Malays along the west coast of the Malay Peninsular and particularly in Negri Sembilan state are ancestrally from the west coast of Sumatra; they are ethnically Minangkabau. They have their own food, housing styles, social customs, and dialect.

And ethnic Malays themselves today live not just in Malaysia but across the Indonesian archipelago, Singapore, southern Thailand, and the southern Philippines. Some Malay nationalists would like to see all these territories carved out and melded into one Islamic, Malay state.

Even Japan, the world's most notoriously racially homogeneous country, has an ethnic Korean minority of around 600,000. One means by which that minority makes its presence felt is by sending remittances to North Korea, where many have their ancestral origins.[6] Few agree with the North Korean government but equally they don't like to see their former compatriots on the brink of starving and so feel obliged to donate money to help them out. The flow of money to North Korea is illegal and it helps to prop up the country's regime.

So it seems that Asia's porous borders today reflect the fluidity of past centuries. And as Asia's economies develop at greatly differing speeds, the amount of migration within the region, both legal but mostly illegal, is accelerating. Advances in transport and communications technology, and international banking, all make it easier than ever before for people to chase opportunities across borders.

One 2005 study estimates that 8.4 million Southeast Asians work abroad, but this figure was largely based on those working legally.[7] For example, the study estimated that 150,000 Burmese are working in Thailand but a more accurate estimate is that some two million Burmese live in Thailand, most illegally. Around a million Indonesians work in Malaysia too, and again many, and probably most, do so illegally. Thousands of Muslim Thais from southern Thailand also work in Malaysia. Mainland Chinese are becoming more obvious in Singapore and Malaysia. Thailand has many Laotians and so on.

People are the main export from the Philippines. They go abroad to work as maids, nurses, gardeners, sailors, and the like. Many work as maids in Hong Kong, Singapore, and the Middle East. Around a million Filipinos leave each year to work as low-paid expatriate labor. And at any one time, around eight million Filipinos are working abroad. Their remittances to the Philippines now amount to more than US$15 billion annually and more than 15% of that country's GDP.[8] And that's just what is recorded officially. Billions more probably arrive as undetected cash in the luggage of returnees or come in via unofficial banking channels.

Singapore is a big recipient of temporary immigrants. It has a population of 4.55 million. But there are not 4.55 million Singaporeans. Almost 20% of Singapore's population, around 900,000, comprises resident foreigners. Many are Western expatriates but many more are Filipinos and Indonesians who work as domestic maids for Singaporeans. And then there are thousands of workers who reside in Malaysia but who cross the causeway between the two countries each day to work, just as thousands flood into Hong Kong from Guangdong each morning, aboard motorcycles and buses, before returning each evening.

Such day commuters are an important source of smuggling too. If each mainland Chinese on a motorcycle arriving into Hong Kong each day brings a carton of cigarettes hidden beneath his leather jacket, that is enough to flood Hong Kong with contraband cigarettes – and that is exactly what is happening.

The World Bank estimated in respect of 2006 that:

- Remittances to India from Indian guest workers abroad accounted for at least US$23 billion, or 3% of India's GDP.
- Expatriate mainland Chinese sent US$22 billion back to China, or about 1% of its GDP.
- Overseas Bangladeshis remitted US$5 billion to Bangladesh, or around 8% of GDP.
- Overseas Pakistanis remitted US$4.5 billion to their country, or 4.2% of GDP.
- Overseas Vietnamese remitted to Vietnam around US$4 billion, accounting for 6.1% of GDP.
- Overseas Indonesians sent some US$3 billion, or 0.6% of GDP.[9]

These figures take account of both legal and illegal migrants and guest workers.

Governments of the region occasionally voice concerns about illegal migration but more often than not they turn a blind eye. Such migrants usually perform the dirtiest, most difficult, dangerous, and low-paid work – not the sort of thing you want your own citizens doing, particularly in, say, a country such as largely middle-class Singapore with its high labor costs. These workers help to keep Asia's economies growing by keeping labor markets flexible and more competitively priced at the low end.

Locals do not especially like large-scale immigration even from neighboring countries. But in Asia, with its weakened democracies, there is little that ordinary people can do about it. In Malaysia, where the government has shown only periodic concern at the number of Indonesian migrants – largely because they are mostly Muslim in keeping with Malaysia's majority Malay population – ordinary Malays tend to see Indonesian guest workers as low-class, aggressive, and abrasive. The popular conception is that Indonesians are responsible for many of the crimes committed in Malaysia, although official statistics show that foreigners commit proportionately fewer crimes than do Malaysians.[10]

In Myanmar, thousands and probably many more Chinese citizens have come in from Yunnan province illegally. Many buy the identity papers of dead Burmese and so not only is the population distorted but so too are figures on its ethnic composition. Mainland Chinese now dominate the commercial centers of northern Burma. As a result, ethnic Burmese have been forced to the outskirts of many centers because of rising property prices.

Of course, not all Asian emigration is to other parts of Asia. Hundreds of thousands of mainland Chinese have streamed into Africa in recent years, following Chinese investment there and various trade and other deals negotiated by the Chinese government. The Chinese are fast resembling the Indian diaspora in East Africa, which was largely expelled during the 1960s and 70s after it came to dominate the commercial centers of East Africa's towns and cities.

In Paris, the bar-tabacs or small bistro coffee shops were once mostly run by the Auvergnats – French families from the mountainous Auvergne region. But today, more than a quarter of all bar-tabacs in Paris are run by ethnic Chinese from China, Cambodia, and Vietnam.[11] The Auvergnats have moved on. Their children are now better educated and they no longer need to work the long hours of a bar-tabac.

In London, Filipinos are overrepresented among staff of the upmarket supermarket chain Waitrose, its sister department store chain John Lewis, and Odeon cinemas. They tend to recruit each other, and have almost transformed these well-known British retailers into Filipino enclaves.

Another factor driving immigration within Asia is Asia's shortage of women. India, China, Bangladesh, Pakistan, and Korea all have a growing problem of surplus males – men who cannot find a wife because there simply are not enough women to go around. Marriage brokers in some of these countries offer to find wives in other Asian countries where there is not such a shortage of women. Marriage brokers in Korea offer to find wives for Korean men in Vietnam, for example. Ethnic Koreans who live in China are another source, as are women from Mongolia, the Philippines, Thailand, Cambodia, and Uzbekistan. As mentioned in the previous chapter, in 2005, marriages to foreigners accounted for an extraordinary 14% of all marriages in South Korea, up from 4% in 2000.[12] So even the racially homogeneous composition of Korea's population is attaining greater diversity.

Brain Drain

Not all migrants within Asia are lower paid workers. Many Asian countries are being stripped of some of their best and brightest talent. Many well-educated Filipinos work abroad – in Hong Kong, the US, and Singapore where they have senior roles in multinationals. Many of the top Malaysian medical and research professionals head to Singapore, Australia, and elsewhere. Many are Chinese and are tired of being made to feel lesser citizens in their own country on account of not being Malay. Many younger, better educated Indonesian Chinese have left Indonesia for the same reason.

China has a brain drain problem too. As pointed out in Chapter 10, research by the Chinese Academy of Social Sciences suggests that of the approximately one million young Chinese who have studied abroad since the 1980s, around two-thirds chose to stay overseas after graduation. Since 2002, more than 100,000 students have gone abroad to study each year but the number of returnees hovers between 20,000 and 30,000.[13]

Much of the emigration from Asia is people leaving for better economic opportunities elsewhere. But some, particularly the better educated, leave because they are fed up with the quality of government under which they must live. Mostly Asia's governments are democratic in name only, and so among Asia's intelligentsia there is a sense that if you cannot change your own government, then the alternative is to physically move to a jurisdiction where the government is more acceptable. To combat this, the Singapore government, for example, attempts to glue its citizens to Singapore by various means, one of which is the "10-year bar," whereby Singapore law automatically cancels the citizenship of Singaporeans who have not returned to Singapore for 10 years.

Undermining Borders and Government

Together, all these factors are breaking down conventional notions of Asian nationality. Huge, new immigrant populations are forming across Asia. These have important implications for businesses and how they market their services. Who would have thought that a sizable population of Vietnamese women should be forming in South Korea? Or that Indonesian makers of traditional toiletries would find a significant market in Malaysia, largely due to illegal Indonesian guest workers there?

And how can governments appeal to nationality when their residents are from many nations? Migration is one of the factors that will weaken the power of Asia's autocratic governments in the coming decades, along with better access to information and communications. But it's not just Asia's low-paid workers who are voting with their feet. More highly skilled workers are too. The drain from countries such as Malaysia and the Philippines is chronic. The governments of these countries should interpret such a drain as a message that they need to lift their game.

Suggestions for Business Strategists and Scenario Developers

▶ Asia's porous borders mean that forecasts for demand of particular products often can be underestimates because they focus on the local market only and neglect to build in the possibility that the product will be smuggled. Even ostensibly ordinary consumer goods such as tooth-paste or instant coffee are smuggled from Malaysia to Indonesia, for example, because of perceptions in Indonesia that the Malaysian-made product is superior in quality.

▶ Both legal and illegal minorities in Asia can lead to large and profitable niche markets for consumer goods and services. The demand for Filipino foodstuffs in Hong Kong, for example, is considerable simply because of the many thousands of Filipino maids who work there.

▶ These émigré communities also require reliable financial services that allow them to quickly and easily remit earnings to their home countries.

▶ Immigration, brokerage, and advice services will continue to be big business around Asia. For example, assisting Malaysian Chinese to leave Malaysia for Australia, New Zealand, the UK, the US, and Canada is already big business in Malaysia. This will only increase as more and more Malaysian Chinese realize that the Malay preferment policies of their government will not be repealed (see Chapter 19).

Notes

1 *Business Times,* "Why the Asian development model may be off track," April 12, 2007.
2 *Business Times,* "S'pore perplexed by Jakarta accusation on trade data," June 14, 2003.
3 *Business Times,* "Jakarta reiterates request for full Singapore–Indon trade data," July 9, 2003.
4 *New Straits Times,* "Navy holds log-laden boat linked to police," July 29, 2004.
5 *International Herald Tribune,* "Asia oil subsidies bring windfall to smugglers," September 27, 2005.
6 *The Economist,* "Pyongyang's cashflow problem," January 13, 2007.
7 Cited in *The Economist,* "Wandering workers," January 20, 2007.
8 *The Economist,* "Migrants' remittances," November 25, 2006.
9 Ibid.
10 *The Economist,* "Wandering workers," January 20, 2007.
11 *International Herald Tribune,* "Face behind Paris 'bistro' counter becomes Asian," May 5, 2005.
12 *International Herald Tribune,* "Also globalized: Asia's marriage market," February 22, 2007.
13 As cited in *Business Times,* "China suffers from worst brain drain in the world," February 14, 2007.

14 Growing Family Breakdown in Asia

▷ Economic growth means more jobs and more money. It also means that more women can afford to leave their husbands. And so families are becoming less important in Asia.

▷ Divorce rates are rising around the region, families are getting smaller, and the number of single-parent families is growing. Is Asia becoming more morally lax? No, just wealthier.

▷ But the change in the structure of families will have important implications for businesses such as residential construction companies and property realtors.

Asia is having smaller families, smaller households, and more divorce. The number of single-person households is growing as is the number of single-parent families. This is the case in East Asia from China to Singapore. Apart from the social implications, this has important business implications, from how marketing is targeted to how the real estate sector should respond to changing household sizes.

The Communist Party in China removed most legal discrimination against women. It made it easier for women to seek divorce. Recent changes have made divorce easier still. A couple need only provide their marriage certificate, identity cards, and residency permits before signing a joint statement that they wish to end their marriage. And so in China, divorce rates have escalated. The rate rose 21.2% in the year to 2005, for example, with 1.61 million married couples (3.22 million people) divorcing during that year.[1]

Divorce rates in Singapore too are rising. In 2005, 6,909 divorces were recorded, more than the previous record of 6,562, set in 2003.[2]

Wives, mistresses, and prostitutes: that sums up the view that many outside Asia have of women in Asia. Nothing could be further from the truth. Women in Asia, particularly in Southeast Asia, play important roles in commerce and public administration. Nor is this anything new or to do with Asia becoming more modern. Women have always played a strong business role in traditional Islamic Malay society, for example.

But aren't women in business contrary to Islam? Not at all. The Prophet Muhammad's first and most cherished wife, Khadijah, was a trader. She came to know Muhammad and provided him with capital so that he could trade on her behalf in Syria. He returned with a good profit and so *she* decided that he would make a suitable husband. She also happened to be 15 years his senior. It's all in stark contrast to the odd interpretation that is Islam as it's practiced today in Saudi Arabia, where women are not even permitted to drive a car.

This is not to say that women are equal to men in Southeast Asia. It's more that men and women have different but well-defined economic roles; areas of competence that are mutually respected. Women still operate most of the stalls in markets across Southeast Asia, for example, which suggests that they operate many and perhaps most of Southeast Asia's small businesses.

Rather than being docile and dependent, social institutions ensure that most women in Southeast Asia are less economically dependent on men than in many other parts of the world, even if their prime role is as a wife.

As in India, dowries were and in some cases remain common across Southeast Asia, but unlike India, dowry wealth is passed from the male side to the female side. Even today, marriages among Malays in Malaysia typically feature the groom's parents giving gifts of gold to the bride. The tradition is sometimes misinterpreted. Rather than the gold representing a "purchase" price, it is in fact a transfer of capital to the bride. She owns it and retains it. It allows her to be less dependent on her husband than would otherwise be the case and, importantly, allows her to more easily exit the marriage if need be.

Accordingly, the idea that family units are sacrosanct in Asia and that a high incidence of marriage breakdown is somehow a Western phenomenon is a fiction. There is a long tradition of divorce in Asia just as there is a long tradition of polygamy and serial marriage.

As it happens, divorce rates in Southeast Asia have been among the highest in the world. Up until the late 1960s, they were in excess of 50% among the Malays and other Muslims of Malaysia and Indonesia.[3] This was not so much because Islam makes it easy for men to get rid of unwanted wives but because the wives usually had some capital of their own; they could afford to leave. It meant that they were not necessarily a husband away from poverty as was the case with many Western women in, say, the 1960s and earlier. Indeed, little opprobrium is attached to being divorced in Malay culture, something demonstrated in mid-2007 when the Malaysian Prime Minister Abdullah Badawi married a divorcee (his previous wife had passed away in 2005).

Also, property was held by both the husband and the wife and administered jointly rather than by the husband alone, as was the case in China and India. Thailand enshrined joint property administration in 1976 with the passing of the Family Law. And among Malay families, the actual control of the family's finances is with the wife. This is the precise opposite to what traditionally has been the case among local Chinese families, in which the man of the house controls everything and the wife remains dependent and even trapped.

Malay children too have tended to have an equal claim in inheritance regardless of sex but with one very important exception: the Minangkabau people of Indonesia and Malaysia. They are matrilineal – the men inherit nothing, everything passes to the daughters. This is still practiced.

When the mother of a Malaysian Minangkabau friend of mine passed away, my male friend inherited nothing even though his mother owned several houses and a rubber tree plantation. It all went to his sister, a situation that he fully accepted. He works as a not particularly well-paid employee in Kuala Lumpur. Meanwhile, his sister manages her inherited businesses back in the town where they are from.

The separate but respected role of women is acknowledged in Southeast Asian motifs and symbolism. Maleness is often associated with white (semen) and the female with red (blood, menstruation.) This suggests one possible origin of the Indonesian flag, which comprises two equal parts – one red and one white – the two distinct but equal elements of the Indonesian nation: men and women. Interestingly, the flag is flown with the red on top.

Women rulers have not been unusual in Southeast Asian history even in ultra-Islamic Aceh. They were seen as less likely to go to war, less likely to tax highly, and less prone to corruption. In recent times, the two East Asian countries that have had female heads of state have been in Southeast Asia: Indonesia (President Megawati Sukarnoputri) and the Philippines (Presidents Aquino and Arroyo). In Malaysia, women form the majority of senior officials in several key economic ministries, and the head of the central bank is a woman.

What this all means is that, traditionally, women are not dependent and subservient. It explains why divorce is not uncommon in Asia, particularly Southeast Asia, and why rising divorce rates now simply represent a return to the historical trend.

Women have traditionally been more dependent on men in China but as mentioned, the Communist Party changed women's roles forever. And today, economic growth is giving women more independence than ever. China's export revolution is very much about women; it is women who staff most of the factories of Shenzhen and near Shanghai that produce the plastic toys, household appliances, and the like that comprise much of China's manufactured exports. Nor do women face overt discrimination in the workplace in China. There is no shortage of companies in Shanghai, for example, with female presidents.

Another aspect is that many women in China will no longer need to marry to secure their economic future. China's export revolution has provided more jobs for women than ever before.

The seedy side of China's economic revolution is the rise of prostitution. It is scarcely possible now to walk more than a few blocks in many Chinese cities most evenings without passing by prostitutes. How many prostitutes are there in China now? Estimates range from 3 to 20 million.[4] Prostitutes in China are both a cause and a consequence of marriage breakdown.

The PR Job

So from where have we got the idea that families in Asia are so sacrosanct? That divorce is somehow restricted to the West? Probably from the Asian values debate that raged prior to the 1997–98 economic crisis. The debate was propagated by some Asian leaders who sought to suggest that Asian cultures were superior to the West in terms of the regard for families, while at the same time seeking to justify authoritarianism in Asia in terms of "Confucian" values. Former Singapore Prime Minister Lee Kuan Yew was a leading proponent as were other Singaporean leaders. But then Lee and his colleagues, while ethnically from the region, were culturally something else.

They were drawn from Singapore's *Baba* Chinese community, a tiny minority acculturated with the local Malay population but historically greatly enamoured with the British colonialists.

The *Baba* proponents of Asian values liked to emphasize the sense of family and community. But just how Asian are these values when it comes to the Chinese population that settled in Singapore in the nineteenth century, with their opium dens, brothels, and gambling houses? They settled into parts of Singapore according to dialect. There was not so much a sense of community but communalism. Families were torn apart by gambling and other vices. Many Chinese of earlier generations were polygamous – they took second and sometimes many subsequent wives.

Sago Lane in Chinatown is still remembered by older Singaporeans as the street of the "death houses" where many old and sick spent their last days. Funeral parlours and shops that sold the paraphernalia associated with death operated from here. Chinatown residents called it Sey Yan Kai or the "Street of the Dead." Death houses were abolished only in 1961. They did not fit in with the values of the *Babas*. Families were supposed to look after their own sick and elderly, not leave them some place else to die.

And, as suggested, Asian values, or at least their contemporary manifestation, were about strong if not autocratic leadership. But submitting to authority was not a strong point of the newly arrived Chinese, who largely came from China's unruly southern provinces. The *Babas*, on the other hand, admired authority – after all that was what the British stood for. In fact, those values that have come to be labeled as "Asian" – strong, patriarchal leadership, frugality, community, and family are the values of Victorian England, the period in which Singapore's *Baba* community had its genesis and which was so admired by them. It was in Victorian England that moral order was linked to economic development and the natural goodwill of men was deemed an unreliable guarantor of order and so was supplanted by a structure of deterrents and incentives to cajole and constrain.[5] These were of course the very sentiments that lay behind the efficacy of strong leadership in the Asian values debate.

And so "Asian" values were not particularly indigenous to Asia, which in any event was mired in banditry, polygamy, concubinage, and narcotics usage, if China is taken as an example. Meanwhile, the Malay community was experiencing some of the highest divorce rates in the world.

Smaller families and divorce are a consequence not of moral breakdown but higher incomes. People divorce because suddenly they can afford to. No longer must they endure an unhappy marriage. So higher divorce rates are a natural consequence of economic growth. Couple this with divorce being made legally easier, as in China, or a long tradition of divorce and female economic independence, as in Islamic Southeast Asia, then it is only natural that divorce in Asia is set to rise dramatically.

Suggestions for Business Strategists and Scenario Developers

► Formal childcare will be a major growth sector in coming decades in Asia. Families are becoming smaller and so there are fewer aunts, cousins, and the like to help with the informal provision of childcare, particularly as more women join the paid workforce and the cost of hiring maids and other domestic help also rises. Increasingly, companies will need to investigate providing workplace childcare facilities as a means of attracting and keeping female employees.

► Smaller families and more single-parent families will mean that more flats and houses with fewer bedrooms will need to be built in Asia.

► More women in work means that there will be a greater demand for convenience and preprepared foods in Asia. Also, more food in supermarkets will need to be packaged into smaller amounts, suitable for one- and two-person households.

► Increasingly, financial products can be targeted to women in Asia. Many have the income and savings now to be interested in such products but also many will be making their own arrangements rather than leaving it up to a spouse.

Notes

1   *Financial Times*, "Divorces on the increase in China," March 2, 2005.
2   *Business Times*, "Number of marriages highest since 2002," September 26, 2006.
3   Reid, A., *Southeast Asia in the Age of Commerce 1450–1680, Volume One: The Lands Below the Winds*, Silkworm Books, 1988, p. 153.
4   *International Herald Tribune*, "Sex industry in China: Obvious but ignored," December 15, 2006.
5   I first made this point in Backman, M., "Asians and Victorian values," *Far Eastern Economic Review*, March 30, 2000.

15 China Builds an Economic Bloc based on Corruption

▷ It's much harder for Western companies to pay bribes now when they do business abroad. Chinese companies are not so constrained. Why would they be? They pay bribes at home. And so China is building an economic bloc of African, South American, and Central and other Asian countries that do business in the way that China does business – with little transparency and plenty of corruption. It means that in coming decades, the world is developing into two economic blocs: a corruption bloc and a bloc that's based on the rule of law.

There's a lot of corruption in China. Not as much as in, say, Africa. But enough to be part of contemporary China's way of life. Transparency International rated China in terms of its perceived corruption at 70 out of 163 countries in 2006 (a rating of 1 implies little or no corruption), meaning that China was perceived as less corrupt than Indonesia or Nigeria but more corrupt than Turkey or Malaysia.[1]

In recent years, China has attempted to invest in the West – for example in Australia and the US – but where it has been making big strides has been in other developing countries, the sorts of countries that Transparency International also rates as corrupt or very corrupt. So how has China managed to become so prominent so quickly in these countries as a business partner? You don't need to be Einstein to work it out: Chinese officials and businesspeople do business in the way they do it at home – they pay bribes. In fact, the evidence suggests that they are even more corrupt than abroad. China is not constrained like the West is in bribing foreign officials. The US has its Foreign Corrupt Practices Act, for example, which means that US nationals who pay bribes to officials of foreign governments or who cause bribes to be paid can be prosecuted back home. Most other OECD countries have enacted similar legislation. And when American, German, or other Western businesspeople are found to have paid bribes abroad, they are prosecuted at home and there is a very public scandal. Not so in China.

China is not a member of the OECD but it has ratified the UN's Convention against Corruption. But essentially, it's a case of "so what." China routinely ratifies Conventions and passes legislation but often it's for international consumption. China's government enforces only those laws that it finds it expedient to enforce. It is very effective at enforcing rules that restrict the media, for example. But when it comes to intellectual property protection laws, these are barely enforced at all. It's the same with the UN Convention against Corruption.

Article 16 of the Convention states that:

> Each State Party shall adopt such legislative and other measures as may be necessary to establish as a criminal offence, when committed intentionally, the promise, offering or giving to a foreign public official or an official of a public international organization, directly or indirectly, of an undue advantage, for the official himself or herself or another person or entity, in order that the official act or refrain from acting in the exercise of his or her official duties, in order to obtain or retain business or other undue advantage in relation to the conduct of international business.

Regardless of what China says it will do, it does not constrain its companies from paying bribes abroad. And most Chinese companies that invest abroad are state-owned or controlled. Indeed, when it comes to paying bribes abroad, out of 30 countries surveyed by Transparency International in 2006, Chinese companies were ranked as second only to India as the most likely to pay bribes overseas.[2]

Not only does China invest in highly corrupt markets where it is at an advantage to, say, Western investors, it invests in places that politically most other investors, particularly from the West, won't touch, such as Zimbabwe under Robert Mugabe, Myanmar under its military regime, and Sudan, whose particularly odious and murderous government China has essentially helped to prop up. Indeed, when US and Canadian oil companies could no longer tolerate Sudan's regime and left the country, China stepped in.

Nigeria is one of the world's most habitually corrupt countries. It is oil-rich but its people are poor. In 2006, the China National Offshore Oil Corporation (CNOOC) paid US$2.3 billion for a 45% stake in an oil and gas field, then one of the largest acquisitions abroad by a Chinese company.[3] An Indian oil company had earlier won the contest for the field but the Indian cabinet blocked the deal because it wasn't obvious who the local Nigerian partner would actually be. The Chinese were not so fussy.

Indeed, at the risk of oversimplifying the situation, the world is separating out into those that can and those that can't when it comes to bribery and corruption. And those that can, like China, have found that they can become significant investors abroad very quickly. It means that in coming decades China will have built an economic bloc based on mutual corruption and bribery. China's emerging foreign aid program is hastening the process.

China Comes to the Aid

Aid and soft loans have become part of China's trade and investment strategy. All countries do this. Japan is a prime example. But China's approach is a little different. Its loans and aid come with few or no strings attached. That seems like a good thing on the face of it. But World Bank and other aid usually is tied to reform. Future lines of credit, for example, are contingent upon anticorruption and other measures being put in place. If the World Bank finds that funds for one of its projects are being misused, for example, then it suspends the project. Not so with China. Its loans and aid come with no provisos or penalties. In fact, the assistance is almost a reward for bad behavior. Some governments now solicit Chinese assistance ahead of help from the World Bank, the IMF, or the Asian Development Bank because they don't need to agree to governance reforms to get it. This undermines the good work that these institutions try to do.

In 2005, China offered Gabon in Africa an aid package that came "without any political conditions," as President Hu Jintao explained in a speech to Gabon's Parliament. In 2006, China offered Cambodia US$600 million in loans, again with no strings attached. Cambodia awarded China oil extraction rights at about the same time. In 2006, China's Export-Import Bank announced that it would give the Philippines US$2 billion in loans each year for the next three years. Angola was rewarded with a no-strings attached US$2 billion line of credit. China's Sinopec and a partner then paid US$2.2 billion for two offshore oil blocks in 2007. Angola ranks at 142 out of 163 on Transparency International's corruption perception list. In Cameroon in Africa, China pledged US$100 million in grants and soft loans and also canceled the country's existing debt to China in 2007. Even Myanmar has been given financial assistance by China, and this when no other aid or multilateral lending agent will any longer lend to it on account of human rights concerns.

China provides direct assistance too, with aid work being contracted to Chinese state-owned companies. The China Shanghai Construction Group, for example, has built a bridge across a tributary of the Mekong River in Cambodia.

On top of this, China is secretive about the aid that it gives. It declines to attend international aid meetings, often chaired by the World Bank, at which various countries' aid projects can be coordinated.[4] But from the developing countries' perspective, China is not patronizing or intrusive. To them, China adopts the position of an equal rather than patron or conqueror. But of course China is not an equal. It has its own agenda.

The One Requirement

China does prefer that *one* requirement be met for its aid, soft loans, and preferential trade and investment: recipient countries must give diplomatic recognition to Beijing and not Taiwan. In the past, Taiwan was able to use its financial muscle to ensure that countries maintained diplomatic relations with it as the rightful government of China rather than Beijing. But now that mainland China has so much economic clout, it is able to effectively buy diplomatic recognition from the holdouts. Liberia switched its recognition from Taiwan to Beijing in 2003, Senegal in 2005, and Chad in 2006. Each was then rewarded with investment and other deals.

Show Us Your Money

So where exactly in the developing world has China been investing? In 1998 and 1999 alone, the China National Petroleum Company (CNPC) spent more than US$8 billion buying into oil and gas concessions in Sudan, Venezuela, Iraq, and Kazakhstan.[5] In July 2003, it paid US$350 million for several oil refineries in Algeria.[6]

In Ecuador, many US and European companies, tired of the persistent corruption at the state oil company Petroecuador, had left the country. So enter China. By the end of 2004, its state oil companies had spent around US$100 million on oil drilling and exploration in the country, apparently untroubled by the working environment.

In Pakistan, China built a port in the coastal city of Gwadar that ultimately will be used to ship Central Asian oil and gas to China. China contributed US$198 million via loans and grants. At least these were the formal sums. Pakistan contributed just US$50 million. Five hundred Chinese laborers worked on site at the peak of the construction in 2002.[7] The port was inaugurated in early 2007.

In Myanmar, CNOOC led a consortium that signed a production-sharing contract for oil and gas exploration with the state-owned Myanmar Oil and Gas Enterprise in 2004. The consortium planned to explore for oil in Myanmar's western Rakhine State.[8] Myanmar is believed to have gas reserves of 87 trillion cubic feet and recoverable oil reserves of 3.2 billion barrels.

In Indonesia, China has invested heavily in the oil sector. It is now Indonesia's largest foreign producer of oil, a sector traditionally dominated by American firms. CNOOC paid US$585 million for oil producer Repsol Indonesia in 2002. It paid another US$275 million for 12.5% of BP's Tangguh project in Irian Jaya in 2003. And PetroChina, a subsidiary of CNPC, acquired Devon Energy in Indonesia for US$262 million also in 2003. CNOOC and PetroChina now account for 12% of Indonesia's daily output.[9] As US investors have pulled out, frequently citing the Indonesian government's lack of resolve in fighting corruption, China has gone in. It's a common pattern.

The Odd Couple: China and Africa

Culturally, East Asians and Africans have little in common. Indeed, the racist attitudes that Africans must endure in many parts of Asia is nothing short of extraordinary, given how some in the Asian media like to portray the West as racist. But China has started to show a lot of interest in Africa, or at least its resources.

Africa has emerged very quickly as a place where China can do business. At least 40 African countries have concluded trade agreements with China. China now sources oil from Nigeria, Equatorial Guinea, Sudan, Gabon, and Angola, which has become China's single largest oil supplier. Copper and cobalt are sourced from the Democratic Republic of Congo and Zambia. Iron ore and platinum come from South Africa, timber from Gabon, Cameroon, and Congo-Brazzaville, and cotton comes from Burkina Faso.[10]

And in 2007, China staged a summit of 48 African leaders in Beijing at which 16 trade and investment deals with China apparently worth US$1.9 billion were concluded. Also, that year, Chinese President Hu Jintao toured eight African countries, announcing more deals and aid as he went.

A wide variety of projects have also been started such as a railway project in Nigeria, a hotel in Algeria, and a mobile telephone network in Tunisia.

China has become a significant business partner of Sudan, geographically Africa's largest country. Sudan's government is a perennial abuser of human rights and stands accused by the world community of ethnic cleansing. But China only sees oil. Prior to China's arrival, Sudan was a net oil importer. China assisted in building wells, refineries, and a massive oil pipeline, from southern Sudan to Port Sudan on the Red Sea, so now Sudan exports oil, mostly to China.

Angola is similarly avoided by much of the West. But in March 2004, China gave it a soft loan of US$2 billion in exchange for 10,000 barrels of oil per day.[11] China has courted Zimbabwe too, the government of which is now an international pariah. China reportedly did a deal worth US$200 million to supply Zimbabwe with fighter jets and other military equipment. Much of Zimbabwe's tobacco crop is now sold to China.[12]

Elsewhere in Africa, China's Huawei Technologies constructed mobile phone facilities in Eastern Algeria in 2003, and in 2004 announced contracts worth US$400 million to service mobile phone networks in Kenya, Zimbabwe, and Nigeria.[13] And in Zambia, Chinese contactors were helping to build a US$600 million hydroelectric plant in 2004.[14] Other Chinese firms spent around US$100 million investing in Zambia's copper industry in 2002 and 2003.[15]

China and Central Asia

China has been doing a lot of business in Central Asia too, much of it oil related. The CNPC bought 60% of Kazakhstan's third largest field, the Aktubinsk field in 1997. A 35% stake in the smaller North Buzachi field was acquired next from a Saudi Arabian company. And China's Sinopec bought 50% of three blocks near the Tengiz field.

The long-planned construction of an oil pipeline to link China with Kazakhstan finally began in September 2004, an extension of the 400 kilometer Kenyak-Atyrau pipeline within Kazakhstan that was completed in 2002. The new pipeline ends at Alashankou, just inside the Chinese border and will have an annual capacity of 70 million barrels. A gas pipeline is likely to follow. China plans to spend billions on new pipelines to then convey the Kazakh oil from Alashankou to its industrialized eastern coast. And in 2006, CNPC paid US$4.2 billion for PetroKazakhstan, a Kazakhstan oil producer.

Suggestions for Business Strategists and Scenario Developers

▶ Scenario planning will need to take account of China's growing presence in Southeast Asia and elsewhere and the fact that China, as a competitor for assets and resources, has methods available to it that are unavailable to most Western companies.

Notes

1 See www.transparency.org.
2 See www.transparency.org. The survey encompassed the views of more than 11,000 businesspeople and asked them to rate foreign firms operating in their country.
3 *International Herald Tribune*, "Chinese oil firm to invest billions in Nigerian field," October 1, 2006.
4 *International Herald Tribune*, "China becomes major player in Asian aid," September 18, 2007.
5 Kleveman, L., *The New Great Game: Blood and Oil in Central Asia*, Atlantic Books, 2003, p. 113.
6 Hale, D., "Will China need a blue water navy to protect commodity markets," background paper published by Hale Advisors LLC, Chicago, January 7, 2004.
7 *International Herald Tribune*, "China builds a port in Pakistan," September 9, 2004.
8 *Business Times*, "Myanmar, Sino-S'pore group sign oil pact," October 25, 2004.
9 *Business Times*, "China firms muscle in on Indon energy industries," July 7, 2003.
10 *The Economist*, "Never too late to scramble," October 28, 2006.
11 *The Economist*, "A new scramble," November 27, 2004.
12 Ibid.
13 Ibid.
14 Ibid.
15 Ibid.

16

Vietnam: The New China?

▷ Per capita income in Vietnam will have likely increased five times in the 15 years to 2010.

▷ Already, Vietnam is one of Asia's open economies, with trade accounting for a far higher proportion of GDP than for China and India.

▷ Wage costs are more competitive in Vietnam than in China. It has a young labor force – Vietnam adds almost a million a year to its population and at least a million to its labor force – and it will stay that way for decades to come.

▷ Vietnam's government is another that is pursuing the economic freedom but little political freedom model.

Vietnam is the next China, or at least that's the claim. But it isn't. Its population at 85 million makes it the world's thirteenth most populous country but it is still nowhere near China's billion-plus population. A more realistic sobriquet is that it is the next Guangdong, which had 110 million people in 2005 – 79 million permanent residents and the rest internal migrants.[1] It means that Vietnam is not set to be an economic colossus on the world stage but it will be a significant economy.

Few economies have traveled as far as Vietnam's in such a short period. The consensus for economic reform permeates its government and the results have been almost immediate. Per capita income in 1993 was a mere US$180. By 2005, it was US$640. By 2010, it is likely to be US$1,000.[2] Economic growth throughout the 2000s has averaged almost 8%. It has gone from being a poor to a middle-income country in just 15 years, a rarely achieved feat. The government aims to make Vietnam an industrial country by 2020. It's an aim similar to other governments in Asia. But Vietnam's seems genuinely determined to put in place the reforms that could make it possible. Clearly, its efforts are yielding results. And in 2006, FDI approvals amounted to US$10.2 billion.

Vietnam remains one of Asia's poorest countries, with income per head less than even India's, but growth has been surprisingly egalitarian. The incidence of poverty in 1990 was more than twice the Southeast Asian average. Now, it is about on a par with the regional average, such that there is now a lower incidence of poverty in Vietnam than in China, India, and the Philippines. Other indicators are positive too. Infant mortality has fallen dramatically, longevity is rising, and almost three-quarters of Vietnamese children of secondary school age attend school, up from about a third in 1990.

Exports have risen dramatically and have grown faster than China's since 1990, albeit from a low base. Vietnam is now one of Asia's most open economies: two-way trade amounts to around 160% of the GDP. That's more than twice that for China and four times the ratio for India.[3]

One of the many risks that Indonesia's economy faces comes from the fact that its exports are not greatly diversified. Malaysia faces this risk too, although to a lesser degree. Vietnam, on the other hand, is developing a diversified range of exports. Commodities are exported, as are agricultural products and, increasingly, manufactures. This will help to insulate the Vietnamese economy against price and market fluctuations in any one product or product group.

Vietnam has quickly emerged as the world's biggest exporter of pepper, the number two exporter of seafood, rice, and coffee and the third largest shrimp exporter. In fact, its rice exports are challenging Thailand as the world's biggest rice exporter and its coffee exports might soon exceed Brazil's, to make it the world's biggest coffee exporter. It has become a big tea exporter too. It even exports tea to India, where it is blended, repackaged, and reexported and no doubt often marketed as Indian tea.

Increasingly, multinational companies are seeing the wisdom of not putting all their eggs into the China basket and so are seeking to diversify away from China. Vietnam is an attractive alternative. Intel, the world's largest semiconductor manufacturer, announced at the start of 2006 that it would build a US$350 million factory. By the end of the year, it had decided to raise its commitment to US$1 billion. It already had two similar factories in China and prudently decided to spread its investment across more markets.

Even Chinese companies are investing in Vietnam. The workforce is capable and competitive – so much so that some mainland Chinese companies have opened manufacturing operations in Vietnam to save up to 30% on labor costs compared with had they stayed home.

Demographics are on Vietnam's side. Whereas China pursued its one-child policy, which is now having dramatic ageing effects on the population, Vietnam pursued a less rigorously applied two-child policy and so it has no such problem. Three-fifths of the population are aged 27 or under. So Vietnam will have a large supply of comparatively youthful workers for years to come. Female participation in the labor force is also high, rising to over 80% for women in their twenties. On top of that, women tend to marry relatively late, typically after they are 25. It all helps to keep Vietnam's labor force competitive.

As it is, Vietnam adds almost a million people to its population a year and at least a million to its labor force and will keep doing so until about 2020. Based on current trends, the population will stabilize at about 120 million around 2050.[4] Population growth and migration to the cities means that Vietnam's cities will almost double in size over the next 20 years, and the cities in the south will grow more quickly due to migration from the north to the more commercially dynamic south.

Vietnam started its *doi moi* (renovation) market reforms in the mid-1980s after an attempt at implementing communism – the last surviving private businesses were nationalized in 1978. It was a disaster and almost plunged the country into famine. The reforms led to a lot of excitement among foreign investors, but the reforms were often half-baked and investors were soon turned off. The government insisted that foreigners have local partners when they invested – usually a state-owned enterprise. Bureaucracy was a nightmare, with endless and seemingly needless permits being required that only encouraged corruption. One 2001 survey found that Vietnam had the most red tape in Asia, being even worse than India.[5] Even Procter & Gamble's Vietnam unit was almost pushed to bankruptcy by arcane government requirements – the first time that the obviously highly solvent consumer goods giant had experienced such problems anywhere. Approvals for investment often were granted but then, when the reality of setting up in Vietnam had sunk in, the applicants did not follow through. Foreigners learned from the experience but so did the Vietnamese government. Foreign investment laws were overhauled. No longer would foreign investors be made to accept a state-owned firm as a joint venture partner in many sectors. More reform came as Vietnam readied itself for WTO membership. This is not to say that there are no longer problems. But of all Asia's developing economies, it is Vietnam and China that have approached economic reform with genuine urgency.

The Star Pupil

Vietnam's government passed an enterprise act in 2000 that permitted small and medium-sized private enterprises to form. Major industries such as telecommunications and power, however, remain dominated by the state sector.

Vietnam joined the WTO in early 2007 to become the organization's 150th member. (Vietnam had hosted the APEC summit in November 2006 – another marker along the road of Vietnam's rehabilitation and return to the world economy.) WTO negotiators had learned from their mistakes when negotiating with China for its entrance to the WTO in 2001 and so more binding and enforceable conditions were applied in respect of Vietnam's entry. The accession agreement ran to 880 pages. What this has meant is that WTO-induced reforms in Vietnam have been even greater compared with China, ensuring plenty of opportunities for foreign investors. The WTO agreement required Vietnam to reduce or repeal many import duties (most goods will ultimately be subjected to zero tariffs or tariffs below 35%), eliminate many subsidies to the textile industry, and allow foreign banks to incorporate wholly owned subsidiaries in Vietnam. China, for example, did not accept fully foreign-owned banks, and instead only allows foreigners to acquire minority stakes in existing banks.

Vietnam's statistics are extraordinarily impressive. Sometimes a little too impressive. Like all developing countries, its statistics-collecting agencies are not well funded and the data is often unreliable. Sometimes statistics are inconsistent with one another. Smuggling also distorts trade statistics.

Farm output is rising but industrial production is rising faster and so agriculture's share of national output is declining. It was about 25% in 2000. By 2010, it will be down to about 15%.[6]

The government has targeted electronics for development as an export sector and has provided generous tax incentives for investors and excellent facilities in industrial parks.

Workers are allowed to join only compliant, party-affiliated trade unions as in China. Wildcat strikes do occur, however, and the government prefers a softly, softly approach rather than a strong-armed one involving troops and strikebreakers. Too often the government gives in to strikers' demands without consultation with employers.

Vietnam is a small net exporter of oil but, by 2014, it will most likely be a net importer. Accordingly, it is planning its first nuclear power plant (see Chapter 7).

Banking will be a huge growth sector. It is a barely tapped sector: Vietnam has 85 million people but only six million bank accounts.[7]

Eighty percent of banking is controlled by five state-owned banks. These are hampered by nonperforming loans typically to state-owned enterprises to which they have been directed to lend. Foreign entrants to the banking sector as per the WTO agreement will dramatically improve the sector's governance and product range and allow greater capital to flow to private enterprise.

Retail is also promising. It's an underdeveloped sector but with a large, young population and per capita income rising rapidly, particularly in urban areas, it is a sector that will show growth in excess of GDP growth.

Vietnam's rapid development has meant that getting good local professional and management staff is difficult and increasingly expensive. Job hopping is rampant and for most foreign companies retaining good staff is one of their biggest challenges. HR problems are compounded by Government Decree 105, which imposes a maximum 3% limit on the number of expatriates who can be employed in an enterprise in Vietnam.

Like China, Vietnam has a huge diaspora spread across the world (the Viet Kieu). Many left in the 1970s as impoverished "boat people." Today, they provide a conduit for family and other network investment and trading to and from Vietnam.

Modernizers Replace More Modernizers

Vietnam's political leadership is shared between the prime minister, the president and the head of the Communist Party. Vietnam underwent leadership change in 2006. But it was a case of the existing reformers being replaced by even more reformers. Nguyen Tan Dung was appointed prime minister after the retirement of his predecessor Phan Van Khai. Aged 58 when appointed, he became Vietnam's youngest prime minister. A technocrat, economically literate and, like Khai, a reformist and a modernizer, he was appointed to carry on Vietnam's economic reforms.

Dung had been appointed one of five deputy prime ministers in 1997. A year later he was also made governor of Vietnam's central bank, the State Bank of Vietnam, where he pushed forward monetary reform and bank mergers, thus giving Vietnam's financial system a more stable foundation.

On becoming prime minister, Dung nominated fighting corruption and developing the Vietnamese economy in a sustainable way as two of his priorities. On one of his first overseas trips as prime minister, Dung met the Pope at the Vatican, the first Vietnamese leader to do so.

But Dung is not the only modernizer. Nguyen Ming Triet, who was appointed president with Dung, also is a modernizer and a reformer. Both are from the country's south. The third member of the power triumvirate, Communist Party chief Nong Duc Manh is another keen reformer with a strong preference for privatizing state-owned assets. Clearly then, there is only one direction for Vietnam – more economic reform and liberalization.

The consensus for economic reform within Vietnam's ruling party is wide. But there is one thing that it will not tolerate – a challenge to its power. It wants economic change but not political change – it's exactly the same position of the ruling parties in China, Malaysia, and Singapore. The media is tightly controlled and surprisingly, given the paucity of technology in Vietnam generally, Vietnam is at the cutting edge of censoring the Internet within its borders (see Chapter 2). And so Vietnam is moving from the malevolent to the benevolent dictatorship model of economic development similar to the Singapore model.

With all the reform, you would think that there was a constituency within the elite pressing for a return to the communist ways of old. Apparently not. The National Assembly urged the government in early 2007 not to slow down the change but to press on with building a market economy. For its part, the government announced that it would accelerate the privatization of hundreds of state-run firms, although not those related to the media, the national railroads, or airlines. When it comes to economic reform, the political elite has sapped the *raison d'être* of the various political dissidents; the demands for change from reformers within the Party are little different from those of the dissidents.

Still Some Challenges

Vietnam has made considerable progress. But there remains much to do. It is more attractive to foreign investors than ever. But it's not yet an easy place to do business. Corruption poses the most serious threat to Vietnam's continued economic development. Transparency International rates Vietnam as one of Asia's most corrupt economies. A former deputy trade minister was jailed for 14 years in early 2007 for taking bribes. He'd used the money to place enormous bets on football matches. Other top officials were also jailed for corruption. Official statistics show that between 2000 and 2004, 12,300 officials were implicated in corruption.[8] But they are only the ones who were caught.

Corruption is endemic. The top leadership at least is thought to be relatively clean of corruption, and indeed behind the push to root out the problem. It's a contrast to some other recent Asian leaders, such as Indonesia's President Soeharto, who was very much part of the problem.

The legal system is based on communist legal theory and French civil law. The courts are antiquated. Property rights are vague and even when they are clear, the courts cannot be depended on to enforce them. This has hampered the development of markets for land; for example you cannot readily sell something even if it is yours when you cannot show clear title.

The taxation system is still very complicated and often vaguely spelt out, leading to inappropriate or sometimes conflicting interpretations on the part of those officials who must implement it. Too often, when specific cases arise, rulings or subordinate legislation are issued, without significant consideration to any guiding principles, further complicating the tax system and creating unfortunate precedents.

One final complication is Vietnam's status as a "nonmarket economy" for WTO purposes. Because of the high degree of government ownership and intrusion in the economy, Vietnam will be defined as a nonmarket economy possibly up until 2017. The main implication of this is that other WTO members need not prove that Vietnamese products are being dumped on their markets prior to applying antidumping measures on them; they merely need to assert it. This makes it difficult for Vietnam to defend itself against punitive antidumping measures. Specific industries will be able to achieve market economy status if they can show that they do not receive government assistance.

Suggestions for Business Strategists and Scenario Developers

▶ Vietnam is a good alternative to China for investment if China is beginning to look too expensive. Also, for companies that have China exposure already, diversifying to Vietnam might be prudent.

▶ Vietnam is still a very poor country. Companies seeking to win favor with government officials should consider making contributions to Vietnam's social development. They can demonstrate that they are good corporate citizens by contributing to schools, healthcare centers, local museums and galleries, and the like. The government remains ostensibly socialist, so appearing too focused on profits is likely to attract criticism.

▶ The requirement to accept a local joint venture partner has been eased and in many cases done away with, so some of the complications of establishing a business in Vietnam have been removed. However, taxation rules and rules that relate to real estate usage are still complicated, confusing, and often contradictory. It means that the rule of law is still very patchy, necessitating good relationships with government officials.

▶ Vietnam's banking and retail sectors show considerable promise for the coming years, particularly in light of Vietnam's ascension to the WTO in 2007.

Notes

1 Xinhua news agency, "Guangdong faces population pressure," February 16, 2005.
2 *International Herald Tribune*, "Vietnam arrives as an economic player in Asia," June 20, 2006.
3 *The Economist*, "Plenty to smile about," March 31, 2007.
4 Population Reference Bureau, "An overview of population and development in Vietnam," 2003.
5 *The Star*, "Vietnam has the most red tape in Asia," February 27, 2001.
6 *The Economist*, "Good morning at last," August 5, 2006.
7 *International Herald Tribune*, "Asians and Europeans get head start in Vietnam," October 27, 2006.
8 *Vietnam Economic Times*, "A tangled web," July 1, 2005.

Burma: The Next Vietnam

▷ Burma is a shambles. But it is the Vietnam of tomorrow, except that it has some advantages that Vietnam doesn't have.

▷ Like Vietnam, development will come irrespective of US-led economic sanctions. Plenty of others are willing to invest, including China, India, Russia, Thailand, and Singapore.

Burma has a population of around 53 million people. That astounds many people. It is a lot of people to be locked away from the rest of the world by economic sanctions that the US and its allies impose on the country to get at its military government. (Compare Burma's population with Cuba's at 11 million or North Korea's at 23 million.)

The reasons for the sanctions arose from multiparty elections that were held in 1990. The National League for Democracy (NLD), the main opposition party, scored a landslide victory, but the ruling junta refused to hand over power. NLD leader Aung San Suu Kyi has been under house arrest almost ever since and her supporters routinely are harassed or jailed.

Ethnically, the population is 68% Burman. The rest comprise minorities, of which the Shan (9%) and the Karen (7%) are the most significant. Overwhelmingly, the people are Buddhist – almost 90%. There are significant Christian and Muslim minorities as well – around 4% each. But although Burma's government has been fighting ethnically based secessionist movements along its northern and eastern borders for decades, there is no evidence of ethnic or religious intolerance among the Burmese themselves.

Burma's economy is a shambles. The ruling generals have little understanding of economics. They grew up in the days of the "Burmese road to socialism." Few have been educated overseas. Similarly, the country's civil servants have little exposure to modern economic theory and practice. And due to the country's isolation, there are few foreign policy advisers to help. As a consequence, the Burmese economy is one of the world's most intruded upon. Regulations, licensing, and permits are changed on a whim. Budget deficits are funded by printing money, which has made the Burmese currency almost worthless, caused hyperinflation, and contributed to the collapse of the banking system. When the country's banks did experience a run in 2003, the government simply didn't know what to do. Most goods and services are perpetually in short supply and the economy is saved from complete collapse by corruption and the black market, which at least help the economy by partly undermining the generals' absurd economic policies.

Almost a third of the government's budget goes to the military. Just 8% is spent on education and 3% on healthcare. Even the most basic medical needs are in short supply.

Believable macroeconomic statistics don't exist. In 2005, for example, the government claimed that the economy grew by 12.6%. The IMF said it was more like 0%. A European Commission report said that it was probably negative.[1] Essentially, no one really knows. Good statistics require well-funded data collection, which Burma doesn't have the money for.

Military figures are the big players in Burma's economy. They are heavily involved in smuggling. China closed the China–Burma border in 2006 to all timber trade, apparently from concern that deforestation in Burma was out of control. In response, members of Burma's military reportedly attacked Chinese migrant workers.[2] Everyone is corrupt. You have to be just to live. It means that anyone can be removed from power and charged with corruption. One's mere existence in Burma is evidence of corruption: it's simply not possible to survive without engaging in some form of black marketeering or corruption. Prime Minister Khin Nyunt was sentenced to 44 years in prison (commuted to house arrest) in 2005 for smuggling, for example. But then his smuggling, or at least that of his supporters, was on a far grander scale and involved cars and gold bullion.

The West's Useless Sanctions

Following the military junta's refusal to give up power after the 1990 elections, the US withdrew its ambassador from Rangoon, opposed

Burma's membership of various multilateral financial organizations, and imposed economic sanctions against Burma, a policy that increasingly has been followed by other Western governments. The aim of the sanctions has been to coerce the military junta to restore democracy and respect human rights.

Why is Burma subject to economic sanctions from the rest of the world? Probably because Burma is not commercially important. Human rights abuses are more comprehensive in China and involve far more people but China is commercially important. Burma rarely executes prisoners, for example. But in China, it's a bloodbath in which thousands are executed each year and more than 50 different crimes carry the death penalty. Nor do people defect from Burma as they do from North Korea. Instead, they simply leave it: there is no shortage of Burmese guest workers in Thailand, Malaysia, and Singapore, for example. And so Burma is the world's whipping boy. It allows the rest of the world and the US in particular to ease its conscience when it does business with the world's other serial human rights abusers.

Burma is not strategically important to the US, so it's a "free kick" politically to take a high-handed approach to the issue. It makes for good headlines and helps to pacify the US domestic human rights lobby, regardless of whether the approach is effective or not.

In any event, the sanctions against Burma haven't worked and won't work. Why? One reason is because Burma has the world's tenth largest natural gas reserves, and it sits in the middle of a region that increasingly is hungry for energy.

Total of France helped to build a pipeline from Burma to Thailand, so now Thailand buys about US$1.2 billion in natural gas from Burma annually. And in 2006, Thailand's state-controlled PTT Exploration and Production announced a "significant" natural gas and oil find in the Gulf of Martaban, off Burma, where it has the sole right to explore for oil and gas in three projects.[3]

In January 2005, India signed an agreement with Burma to build a pipeline across Bangladesh to import Burmese gas.

China's National Development Reform Commission approved plans in 2006 to build a pipeline that will carry Middle East oil from a deepwater port off Sittwe across Burma to China's Yunnan province, so that China's oil will have an alternative route to being shipped through the Malacca Straits.

Also in 2006, Russia's state-owned Zarubezhneft oil company was awarded a contract to explore Burma's offshore oil and gas reserves. Big contracts were also given to China's National Petroleum Corporation.

Indeed, rather than isolating Burma, the US and the rest of the West have handed it on a platter to those countries that are less fussy about who they deal with. And it relates not just to oil and gas. In 2006, Burma recorded US$6 billion in foreign investment – much of it from one Thai hydroelectric project.

In 2007, Indonesia banned sand exports to Singapore which Singapore uses for land reclamation, so Burma offered to export sand, cement, granite, and other construction materials to Singapore instead.[4]

Another reason why the West's sanctions against Burma are futile is because Burma is a country that has deliberately sought isolation for much of its modern history. In 1962, the then military government voluntarily sealed off the country, banned most foreign trade and investment, nationalized businesses, and banned most tourism. It stayed that way until the early 1990s. It means that Burma is a country that is used to making do on its own.

The West persists with its sanctions to force Burma to become a democracy. But the main preoccupation of Burma's military rulers is the preservation of the state. It is something that they have in common with most other Asian governments: to stamp out secessionist tendencies even when letting go of the odd renegade region would make more sense, commercially and politically. Witness China over Tibet and Indonesia over Aceh and East Timor. Defeating separatism is a unifying cause célèbre: it helps to unify the military, ensures its centrality in national affairs, and provides an excuse to suspend individual liberties and political freedoms while separatist emergencies are being handled.

The Burmese government has reached settlements with 17 of Burma's separatist movements but not all. For example, eight Shan politicians were arrested and sentenced to prison terms ranging up to 106 years in 2004, apparently to discourage other ethnic groups from pursuing independence. In the eyes of the generals, the risk that their country might splinter justifies the suspension of personal liberty and human rights. Democracy isn't even on their radar, quite legitimately they feel, while large parts of the country are threatening to pull away.

The Burmese army is around 400,000 strong. It is battle hardened from decades of fighting insurgency movements. And so it is one of the biggest and most experienced armies in the world. It has also been rearmed thanks to the money that Burma has earned from selling natural gas. Technical assistance, sophisticated weapons, and military IT have come from China and Singapore too. All this means that the military will be even harder to dislodge from power.

Meanwhile, little that prodemocracy leader Aung San Suu Kyi has done has yielded tangible benefits for her people. She remains under house arrest. Her patient and peaceful resistance won her a Nobel Peace Prize and worldwide admiration but unfortunately achieved little else.

Advocates of sanctions uncritically cite the case of South Africa where economic sanctions did help to end apartheid. But South Africa is not Burma. It was industrialized, had been well connected to the rest of the world, had a significant middle class, and was dependent on international trade. None of this is true of Burma.

Burma was admitted to the Association of Southeast Asian Nations (ASEAN) in 1998. Since then the other nine ASEAN countries have either done little to promote change in Burma or have openly supported the regime by investing in Burma. Partly this is because they lack the clout or the diplomatic skills to effect change. But also they would rather see the government evolve than be removed. They don't buy into the sanctions argument and don't see why they should follow the US approach, which they genuinely and correctly see as fundamentally flawed.

Any attempt to embarrass Burma's rulers is pointless. They simply don't care. The UN General Assembly has passed 16 consecutive resolutions calling for change in Burma. The regime has ignored each one. Nor does it have plans to go anywhere. Its draft constitution contains a requirement for the president to have had 15 years of military service, a third of the parliamentary seats to be reserved for the military, and its budget to be placed outside civilian control. This largely mirrors Indonesia under the military dictator Soeharto, of whom Burma's military rulers were an admirer.

The Burmese government formally moved the administrative capital from Rangoon to Pyinmana, which was renamed Nay Pyi Taw, a hitherto largely empty location, about 320 kilometers north of Rangoon, in 2005. The move was formalized on the 11th day of the 11th month and involved 11 ministries, underscoring the belief in astrology and numerology that is common in Burma. No one is sure why the government chose to relocate the capital. Historically, Burma's kings often relocated their capitals on the advice of astrologers or to signal what they regarded as some sort of epochal shift. Some observers felt that the government felt less vulnerable to outside attack than if it stayed in Rangoon. If that is correct, the relocation was misconceived. The central government is now more open to attack from guided missiles from, say, a US-led force eager to avoid civilian casualties than would be the case if an attack had to be made on Rangoon.

But, in short, the junta will never voluntarily give up its rule. That's not the Asian-Confucian way. The way forward is not regime change but regime modification. Consider Vietnam. It has gone from pariah to poster boy in little more than a decade. It wasn't necessary to overthrow the Communist Party to bring about huge economic reform. Instead, reformers have been allowed to rise from within. It's the same with China. And it is the most obvious and likely path for Burma. So far, threatening Burma's rulers has only driven them into a bunker, or at least Nay Pyi Taw. The West will engage them because there is no other option. The case of Libya and its leader Muammar Abu Minyar al-Qadhafi shows that even the most roguish leaders and states can be welcomed back to the international community. Eventually Burma will be open for business. And when it is, it promises to be a bonanza.

A Modern Burma

Why does Burma have so much potential? Culture is extremely important. Some cultures simply are more adept at commerce than others. Rangoon has a buzzy feel. People hurry about. They are self-confident and busy. They don't act like a people isolated from the world by sanctions. The culture is one that is ready for business. It is not like Jakarta, for example, which is congested more than busy and the people on the streets languidly plod around amid a general atmosphere of pathos. You get the feeling that when Burma does open up, when the political situation changes, and Burma's leaders are welcomed in from the cold in the way that Vietnam's leaders have been, then Burma will be something quite special.

What else does Burma have going for it? Consider these factors:

- As mentioned, Burma has the world's tenth largest known natural gas reserves.
- Burma is the world's biggest producer of gem-quality jade and rubies.
- Other natural resources include petroleum, tin, zinc, copper, tungsten, lead, coal, marble, and limestone.
- Burma, unlike neighboring Thailand, retains enormous forests of timber.
- Burma has almost 2,000 kilometers of coastline and so has considerable fishing rights.
- Burma has a critical mass population – with around 53 million people, the population is not too small such that labor costs will rise any time

soon (unlike Malaysia), nor too large relative to other resources to hinder development (as is the case with India).

- Burmese culture is industrious and outward looking.
- English is still widely spoken.
- The legal system is based on English common law, unlike Vietnam.
- Strategically, Burma is located near major Indian Ocean shipping lanes. As it is, Burmese crew many of the merchant ships that fly flags of convenience around the world. And Burma shares borders with Bangladesh, China, India, Laos, and Thailand.

On top of these factors, Burma has astonishing tourism potential. The stupas on the plains around Pagan in the north are stunning as is the massive gilded Shwedagon Pagoda complex in Rangoon. Rangoon's museums contain some of the most fabulous jewel encrusted regalia in Asia and Burmese food is distinct and complex – a pleasing blend of Thai and Indian styles. Sanctions and years of isolation have helped to preserve Burma. It is like a large, living museum itself. But not for much longer.

Suggestions for Business Strategists and Scenario Developers

▶ When will Burma be open to all for business? It's hard to say. But just as the reunification of North and South Korea is inevitable, Burma rejoining the world community is inevitable too. And when it does, investors will find plenty to interest them.

▶ Potential investors would do well to educate themselves now about what Burma potentially has to offer so that when they are able to invest they can hit the ground running.

Notes

1   *International Herald Tribune*, "In Myanmar, economy is shrouded in mystery," April 16, 2005.
2   AFP, "Japan's position on Myanmar irks US," June 4, 2006.
3   *International Herald Tribune*, "Thailand announces Myanmar oil find," August 7, 2006.
4   *Business Times*, "Myanmar could supply sand, granite," April 4, 2007.

Does Indonesia Have a Future?

> ▷ Wages are low in Indonesia but, due to corruption, it is a costly place to do business.
>
> ▷ Indonesia's economy has become less important relative to the world's other economies. It is likely to become even less important.
>
> ▷ Indonesia's saving grace has been its oil and gas reserves but these are running out.
>
> ▷ Indonesia is an OPEC member but is on the verge of being a net oil importer and possibly being expelled from OPEC.

Tenaga Nasional, Malaysia's state-controlled power company, announced in 2007 that it would sell its coal mines in Indonesia and would do so at a loss of around US$60 million. Coal mining is not a business that Tenaga knows well, said its CEO, and in future the company would stick to core activities. He added that in future the company would invest its money only in countries where it is "comfortable" working.[1] It was an extraordinary indictment: a government-controlled company from Malaysia admitting that it can't operate in Indonesia. If a Malaysian company can't, then what sort of company can?

Indonesia does not offer an easy business environment. Its outdated, obscure Dutch colonial laws are slowly being updated and overhauled. But the slowness has attracted criticism from various international agencies, including the World Bank, the IMF, and the Japan International Cooperation Agency. Meanwhile, foreign investment in Indonesia has ebbed away. Investment approval figures often obscure actual investment: investors often get approval for investment but then choose not to follow through. Indonesia used to excite foreign investors. Now they invest there if they feel they have to. The buzz has gone.

World Bank data even showed that when ranking the world's economies by their average GDPs for the five-year period 1980–84 with that for 2001–05, Indonesia's position among the world's economies actually fell three places, meaning that the relative size of Indonesia's economy actually fell.[2]

Terrorism, natural, and man-made disasters have all taken their toll on confidence in Indonesia's future. The disasters themselves are one thing but how the Indonesian government responds to them has exposed many weaknesses to both domestic and foreign audiences.

The first few months of 2007 were particularly horrific. A state-owned Garuda plane crash came within weeks of another major plane crash, two major ferry sinkings, and several train derailments. Shortcomings exposed other weaknesses; for example the names of several victims of the Garuda crash were not even on the flight list – they had been flying on tickets bearing other people's names.[3] This when air security due to the threat of terrorism is supposed to be high.

What are the challenges facing Indonesia's economy in the coming decades? The biggest challenge is to bring back foreign investors – those who are keen to be a part of a dynamic, growing economy by developing new assets, rather than investors who simply acquire cheap, existing assets sold by those who are exiting. Reducing corruption and enhancing transparency is the key. Is Indonesia ready to rise to the challenge? Nothing so far suggests that it is.

Indonesia: A High-cost Place to do Business

Indonesia has low wages. But it is a high-cost place to do business. The reason is the sheer hassle of getting anything done. Transparency is low, which means that confusion is high. Too many have a vested interest in the maintenance of low transparency. The more confusion there is, the more opportunities for "consultants" and "facilitators" to inject themselves into the equation to help businesspeople through the mess. And the more red tape and forms there are to be filled out, the more opportunities there are for officials to demand bribes. Indeed, corruption has become so bad in Indonesia that any government service that is supposed to be provided without charge will only happen if a payment is made. This is the case almost without exception. The ports provide one of many examples. The Transport Ministry released a report in mid-2005, which found that illegal fees levied at Indonesia's major ports actually exceeded the legal charges.[4] And that's just at the ports. Factor in levies and unofficial payments throughout the economy and Indonesia starts to look very expensive.

In its annual surveys of corruption perceptions, Transparency International rates Indonesia as one of the most corrupt countries on earth. Corruption pervades everything. Even schoolchildren and religious pilgrims are ripe for targeting. In 2004, the World Bank asked the Indonesian government to repay a US$10 million loan that had been given for the purchase of school textbooks, after an investigation found that the money had largely been stolen.[5] And in 2006, Said Agil Munawar, the country's religious affairs minister from 1999–2004, was jailed for five years for his role in misappropriating funds that his ministry had collected from ordinary Indonesians so that they could go on the haj to Mecca.[6]

One of the great problems of grappling with corruption in Indonesia is that Indonesians themselves have flexible attitudes to it. Surveys have shown that Indonesians tend to define corruption in terms of quantity, meaning that it's only corruption if a lot of money is improperly taken. Many also see it almost as a right or as natural that those in power should use their positions to enrich themselves. Public disgust only arises if they are too greedy.

Legally, corruption has tended to be defined only as instances where the state's finances are harmed. Bagir Manan, chief justice of Indonesia's Supreme Court, even said in 2006 that if the state gets stolen government money back, then there is no need to hunt those who stole it.[7] According to the law, essentially Manan was correct. But his background instilled little confidence. He was appointed chief justice in 2001 despite having no judicial experience. He had been a director general in the Ministry of Justice under President Soeharto and a former administrator of Soeharto's Golkar Party.

Greater democracy in the post-Soeharto era has introduced new forms of corruption. Political power is now more decentralized compared with the Soeharto years – there is now a wider range of people who must be bribed. There are now many more political parties and these also need money. It emerged at the 2007 trial of one former minister that he had siphoned off funds from his ministry and passed it to several political parties, for example.[8]

Most judges, and everyone else connected with the legal system, are corrupt. Many lawyers function as conduits for bribes to judges, prosecutors, and police. This means that the law is applied in a haphazard fashion – not according to precedent or policymakers' intent but as if by a sealed-bid auction. Again, this raises the costs of doing business in Indonesia. But the costs are not restricted to inappropriate payments to legal officials. Entire investments of many millions can be transferred on a whim by judges or held up for years while ownership matters are resolved. Many examples of this have received publicity outside Indonesia. One lesser known example involved the UK's agrobusiness group Rowe Evans Investments. It signed a contract in 2002 to buy a plantation in North Sumatra from a local politician for US$2.3 million. But a local court annulled the contract in 2004 and ordered that the plantation be returned to the politician, a decision that "shocked" the UK company. The company said it would rigorously appeal the decision and decided to put future investment in Indonesia on hold.[9] Such decisions, whereby millions of dollars in assets are transferred without due consideration, are not uncommon.

Newmont Mining, the world's second largest gold miner, came unstuck in Indonesia after local police accused it of polluting a bay near its operations on Sulawesi Island. A police report showed that mercury and arsenic levels in the bay were well above national standards. Police initially jailed seven Newmont executives in Indonesia and then focused their charges on the expatriate head of Newmont in Indonesia. Prosecutors wanted him jailed for three years. However, no other tests could replicate the police tests, including tests undertaken by the Australian government's scientific organization, the CSIRO, the WHO, and other Indonesian government agencies.[10] Ultimately, Newmont and its head were acquitted.

Oil and Gas

The oil and gas sector is Indonesia's most important. Indonesia has more than 80 oilfields spread across more than 140,000 square kilometers. It has done well from oil and gas. Or at least it should have. Proceeds from the sector have helped to keep the country afloat, while its political leaders and government officials have grotesquely mismanaged the national economy. But unfortunately, legal uncertainty and corruption in the sector, as in Indonesia generally, have been so bad that Western oil companies have shied away from extending their operations. Anecdotally, Western oil company officials view corruption as having worsened since the fall of President Soeharto in 1998. Consequently, the sector now suffers from profound underinvestment – old oil wells are drying up faster than new ones are being found. And so few new wells have been drilled that oil production has fallen by a third in the past decade – from around 1.6 million barrels in 1991 to less than 1 million now. In June 2006, crude oil production hit a 35-year low, when already low production was affected by rains that disrupted drilling in Borneo and the temporary closure of fields in Sumatra for maintenance. Production fell to an average of 908,000 barrels per day during the month, the lowest monthly figure since 1971.[11]

Indonesia is OPEC's second smallest member. The reality is that it should no longer be a member. It has been unable to meet its OPEC production quota since 2002. Not only that, its position as an oil exporter has gone into reverse – the country was a net oil importer for some of 2006, for example. Some in Indonesia even called for Indonesia to voluntarily leave OPEC simply to save the almost US$2 million annual membership fee. This has been a tragedy for Indonesia. Between 2005 and 2007, oil prices stayed at historic highs but Indonesia was unable to benefit.

Part of the problem is that domestic oil consumption is too high, on account of massive government subsidies to the retail price of gasoline and kerosene. A 29% increase in the retail price of gasoline and diesel in early 2005 took the price to around 26 cents a liter, a minimal price by world standards.[12] Large street protests occurred in response.

The Indonesian government hopes to restore oil and gas production to previous levels, particularly as it accounts for about 30% of the state budget. It has awarded new exploration leases. A large new oilfield was found at Cepu, in eastern Java in 2001, but development of the field was only approved in 2006 after five years of wrangling between the state-owned oil company Pertamina and ExxonMobil, the oil company that actually found the field. And when production does come on stream, probably in 2009, it is likely to add 165,000 barrels per day. That's a significant but not a great amount.

Indonesia has been the world's largest exporter of liquefied natural gas (LNG). But again, its fields are running out faster than new ones are being found. Corruption and legal and political uncertainty again have hampered new investment. Simply, there are better places to do business. In 2006, the US oil and gas company Chevron, which operates the world's largest LNG plant on the Indonesian part of Borneo island, was unable to meet commitments to customers in Japan, South Korea, and Taiwan because it could not secure enough gas locally. Qatar is the obvious new competitor. It has become the world's biggest LNG supplier and some of Indonesia's traditional LNG buyers have switched to Qatar. Japan, for example, which traditionally has bought 40% of the world's LNG production, a quarter of it from Indonesia, already buys almost 40% of the LNG produced by Qatar.

Indonesia's emerging democracy has given new voice to regional and sectional interests. In 2006, for example, even Vice-president Jusuf Kalla joined calls for gas from Borneo to be diverted from exports and existing supply contracts to other parts of Indonesia, further damaging Indonesia's reputation as a reliable supplier.[13] Such calls have also frightened off investors. Developing new fields is phenomenally expensive. Investors do not want to do this only to be told that they must sell some of the gas produced at lower prices into domestic markets rather than to better paying customers such as Japan.

The consequence of all this is that FDI in Indonesia has been in long-term decline. Many former investors such as BP, ExxonMobil, and Rio Tinto have reduced their exposure, citing concerns with legal certainty and continuing corruption.[14] Correspondingly, many of Indonesia's brightest young graduates, many who are ethnically Chinese, have left Indonesia for Singapore, the US, and Australia. Businesspeople have left too. Typically, they are ethnically Chinese and left Indonesia for Singapore in the wake of the anti-Chinese rioting in 1998. Many still operate their Indonesian businesses from Singapore. Others have cashed out of Indonesia or reduced their Indonesia exposure. Merrill Lynch and Capgemini in their first *Asia-Pacific Wealth Report* concluded that at the end of 2005, Singapore was home to 18,000 high net worth individuals of Indonesian origin.[15] Collectively, they held US$87 billion in financial assets. It says a lot about a country when the heart of its business community actually chooses to live abroad.

Suggestions for Business Strategists and Scenario Developers

▶ Downward pressure on the Indonesian rupiah is likely to be a long-term trend, unless Indonesia is able to better diversify its export base and increase its production of oil and gas. The Indonesian economy will also be less resilient to external shocks and general downturns.

▶ Corruption in Indonesia is very bad and possibly worsening. Many Western investors will find that they simply cannot invest in Indonesia in any meaningful way and still comply with the laws in their home countries.

▶ Petty corruption is rife and should investors establish operations in Indonesia, they need to build all the facilitation fees that they will need to pay into their cost structures when attempting to estimate future earnings.

Notes

1 *Business Times*, "Malaysia's Tenaga quits Indonesia coal business," May 2, 2007

2 *The Economist*, "Economy rankings," December 16, 2006.

3 *Business Times*, "Pall over Garuda and Indonesia," March 15, 2007.

4 *Business Times*, "Stop corruption – or say goodbye to FDI, enterprise," May 10, 2005.

5 *International Herald Tribune*, "Briefings – Asia," September 30, 2004.

6 *Business Times*, "Former Indonesian religion minister jailed in graft case," February 8, 2006.

7 Verity, A., "Skewed justice in Indonesia's tainted courts," *Asia Sentinel*, August 21, 2006.

8 *The Age*, "Jakarta corruption on trial," May 19, 2007.

9 *Business Times*, "FDI slide signals further problems for Indonesia," May 20, 2004.

10 *The Age*, "Newmont Indonesia chief cleared over pollution," April 25, 2007.

11 *Business Times*, "Indonesia's crude oil output falls to 35-year low," July 19, 2006.

12 *International Herald Tribune*, "Indonesia misses out on oil market windfall," March 21, 2005.

13 *International Herald Tribune*, "Natural gas running low in Indonesia," August 10, 2006.

14 Op. cit. *Business Times*, May 20, 2004.

15 Merrill Lynch and Capgemini, *Asia-Pacific Wealth Report*, 2006.

19 From Malaysia *Boleh* to Malaysia *Bodoh*?

▷ Malaysia has a lot going for it, so why isn't it doing much better than it is? Essentially, Malaysia's oil and gas reserves have protected the country from the effects of wasteful government polices. But what is going to happen when the oil runs out?

▷ One luxury that Malaysia has persisted with is its race preferment polices that see the Malay population given opportunities that Malaysian Chinese and other non-Malays do not receive. Many assume that these will be phased out. They will not – they will continue indefinitely.

Malaysia is in trouble. It shouldn't be. Few countries arrived at independence with so much going for them in terms of factor endowments – ample water supply, a strategic location on international shipping lanes, huge timber reserves, big reserves of tin, oil and gas, the prospects of growing tropical oils such as palm oil, and a legal system based on English tort law. And in many respects Malaysia has done well. But it could have done so much better. Instead of being successful, too often Malaysia has tried to buy the ornaments of success – the world's tallest building, an unnecessarily large international airport, and so on. But in 2025, the one commodity that has paid for much of this – oil – is due to run out. By then, Malaysia's population will have risen by more than 50% from the current level of 23 million to more than 35 million. As it is, Malaysia will become a net oil importer in 2010 if current consumption trends continue.[1]

Already, foreign investors can see that something is up. No longer is Malaysia as attractive to them as it once was. UN figures show that from 2004 to 2005, foreign investment in Malaysia fell by 14%. And this was when the world economy was enjoying one of its longest periods of growth ever. This should have served as a warning tremor of a major earthquake to come.

A Reuter's report at the end of 2006 said:

> Foreign investors have little enthusiasm for Malaysia but it has little to do with traditional business factors such as production costs. Rather their lack of interest has more to do with a litany of more esoteric issues such as mountains of red tape, opaque decision-making, affirmative action policies, a lack of skilled workers and hints of religious tension.[2]

Even tiny Singapore with few natural resources received around six times the FDI that Malaysia did in 2006.

But what is Malaysia's response? Once again, in late 2006, Malaysia was at it again, arguing about what proportion of the economy each of its two main races – the Malays (who with indigenous races comprise around 60% of the population) and the wealthy Chinese minority (which comprises about 24%) – owns. It's an argument that's been running for 40 years. That wealth and race are not synonymous is important for national cohesion, but it's time for Malaysia to move on. It's a tough world out there and there can be little sympathy for a country that prefers to argue about how to divide up wealth rather than get on with the job of creating it.[3]

One problem is that Malaysia's main racial groups really only mix socially and intermarry at the upper echelons of Malaysian society. This group tends to be well off, well traveled and well educated, and often of mixed race and culture. The women tend to wear elegant *kebaya*, be they Chinese, Malay, or some mix. Prime Minister Abdullah Badawi is an example. His maternal grandfather was a Chinese Muslim. His late first wife was half-Japanese. And he remarried in 2007, marrying a Muslim convert from a Portuguese Eurasian Catholic family. While this sort of intermarriage is common among the elite, it is yet to take root among ordinary Malaysians. Malaysia's elite has become racially and culturally almost a distinct group compared with ordinary Malaysians who maintain their separate racial identities, thus perpetuating the endless focus on race and wealth distribution.

The long-held aim is for 30% of corporate equity to be in Malay hands, but the figure that the government uses to justify handing over huge swathes of public companies to Malays but not to other races is absurd. It bases its figure on equity valued not at market value but at par value.

Many shares have a par value of, say, $1 but a market value of $12, which means that the government figure (18.9% is the most recent figure) is a gross underestimate. So when a paper by a researcher at a local think tank came up with a figure of 45% based on actual stock prices, all hell broke loose.[4] The paper was withdrawn and the researcher resigned in protest.

"Malaysia *boleh*!" is Malaysia's national catchphrase. It translates to "Malaysia can!" and Malaysia certainly can. Few countries are as good at wasting money. The national obsession seems to be to extract the nation's natural resources and to fritter away the proceeds on projects aimed at helping to alleviate what can only be described as a national inferiority complex.

Petronas, the national oil company, is well run, particularly when compared to the disaster that passes for a national oil company in neighboring Indonesia. But in some respects, this is Malaysia's problem. The very success of Petronas means that it is used to underwrite all manner of excesses.

The KLCC development in central Kuala Lumpur is an example. It includes the Twin Towers, the tallest buildings in the world when they were built, which was their point. It certainly wasn't that there was an office shortage in Kuala Lumpur – there wasn't.

Malaysians are very proud of these towers. But they scarcely had anything to do with them. Literally, the money for them came out of the ground in the form of oil wealth and the engineering was contracted out to South Korean companies. They don't even run the shopping center that's beneath them. That's handled by Australia's Westfield. And when they were completed, businesses all over town were pressed to move into them – to do their "national service" – so that Malaysians collectively would not look silly on the international stage for having gone and built the world's tallest buildings only to have them stay empty. But this is the sort of harassment that foreign companies simply don't need.

Other examples of government waste and abject silliness abound. For example, the government announced in mid-2006 that it would spend M$490 million on a sports complex near the London Olympic site so that Malaysian athletes can train there and "get used to cold weather." But the *Summer* Olympics take place in the summer. So what is the complex's real purpose? The dozens of goodwill missions by ministers and bureaucrats to London to check on the center's construction and then on the athletes while they train might provide a clue. There is a small Harrods outlet in Kuala Lumpur but let's face it, the range is better in London.

Bank bailouts, a Formula One racing track, an entire new capital city – Petronas has paid for them all. It's been an orgy of nonsense that Malaysia can ill afford. What's particularly worrying is the degree to which the Malaysian government's annual budget is dependent on Petronas. For the year to March 31, 2007, it paid more than RM48 billion (US$14 billion) in taxes, dividends, royalties and export duties to the federal government, representing a whopping 35% share of the government's estimated budget for the year. On top of that Petronas also subsidized gas prices to power producers and some other industrial users to the tune of RM16 billion (US$4.7 billion).[5] Not only do these subsidies mask the degree to which much of the edifice of the Malaysian economy is dependent on this one company, such subsidies potentially expose Malaysian exporters to a challenge under WTO rules which generally prohibit such apparently state-directed subsidy. Petronas has growing investments abroad but the earnings from these will generate less government revenue per dollar than the company's earnings derived from within Malaysia. Host governments will have first call on taxes on Petronas' earnings from abroad, for example.

The one intrusion into the economy that has had its merits is the race preferment policies of the New Economic Policy (NEP) and its successor policies. It has been good for the Malays and for the Chinese. (It has not been so good for Malaysia's Indians.) The NEP has broken the link between great wealth and race. It is no good for any country if all the very rich people belong to one ethnic group. That's a recipe for disaster.

Many Malay businesses have been given contracts and opportunities that they would not have had otherwise. Quite often there has been waste and inefficiency in this. Some waste and some inefficiency is a reasonable price for Malaysia to pay, given the ethnic makeup that history has handed it.

It's difficult to say whether the NEP has hurt Malaysia's competitiveness. The NEP education policies have seen many Malays receive higher education. That is good for competitiveness and for investment. It has meant that Malays are better and more useful employees than would otherwise be the case, for example. Overall, what is important is balance.

Exit Malaysia

One of the greatest risks for Malaysia's future prosperity is migration. As hundreds or thousands of low-skilled guest workers pour in from Indonesia and Myanmar, many of Malaysia's brightest have left. Most, but not all, are ethnically Chinese who find the political climate stifling but also the tolerance of sloppiness and preference for national self-aggrandizement in the

face of so much evidence to the contrary simply irksome. The 2006 UMNO
General Assembly was the last straw for many Malaysian Chinese. Many
were deeply offended by the imagery of Education Minister Hishammuddin
Hussein appearing before the Assembly waving a kris (Malay sword) and
intoning that Malay privileges would continue to be protected. In the weeks
after the conference, Kuala Lumpur-based immigration consultants were
flooded with enquiries from local Chinese who wanted to migrate to countries like Australia, New Zealand, and Canada.[6]

Most of Malaysia's Chinese grimly hang on, assuming that eventually
the preferment policies that see Malays given most government contracts,
most university places, and huge share allocations will be phased out.
Certainly, the measures were put in place for a good reason – to sever the
link between race and wealth. But Malaysia is a democracy by and large.
And now that these policies are in place, the Malay majority will simply
never vote for their removal or any party intent on removing them. This
means that non-Malays in Malaysia must either put up with the race
preferment policies indefinitely or leave. It's a sad outcome for Malaysia's
Chinese, particularly when they almost invariably now describe themselves as Malaysian rather than Chinese and usually quite proudly so. And
when they have learned Malay and largely accepted the race-based bias,
which is aimed squarely at them, in the interests of nation building.
Collectively, they await a pay day, when the preferment policies will be
removed and all Malaysians will be treated equally by their government.
That day isn't going to come.

Transparency? No Thank You, We're Malaysian

Getting a clear picture of what is really happening in corporate Malaysia is
often impossible because of the use of endless nominee companies. This is
particularly the case when government contracts are involved. Presumably
the receipt of government contracts is a source of some embarrassment
and needs to be hidden.

The government adds to the sense of impropriety by using the Official
Secrets Act. This Act was drafted in 1972 to protect state secrets in matters
of national defense and security. But the government now uses it to avoid
disclosing anything embarrassing or which might appear improper –
certainly subjects for which the Act was never intended. For example, in
2006, the government decided to raise the tolls on many toll roads. From
an economist's perspective, this was a good thing because Malaysians use
cars far too much and Malaysian roads are too congested. But the problem

was that the agreement between the government and the private company given the toll concessions was declared a secret document under the Official Secrets Act, meaning that anyone who came into its possession, much less disclosed its contents, was liable for prosecution. The government's agreement with private water companies has similarly been declared a state secret. It's the sort of practice that increasingly is turning foreign investors off Malaysia.

By early 2007, Malaysia had decided that it would build a new metropolis in its southern Johor state to "rival" Singapore and Hong Kong. Yet again, Malaysians failed to understand that there's more to making a great city than pushing together concrete blocks and steel struts. What matters are its soft institutions: a pro-business, transparent, corruption-free environment – harassing businesspeople with quotas, unwritten criteria, and endless, implied petty demands from government officials for gifts and favors done for nephews, cousins, and the like does not.

As Tunku Abdul Aziz, former head of the Malaysian chapter of Transparency International, said, Singapore and Hong Kong are not great cities by accident:

> For us, so used to and comfortable with our slapdash approach to doing things, it will require a complete culture change, which in turn can come about only if there is an unequivocal commitment by the government to facilitate necessary change management. Nothing less than a thoroughgoing reform of our legal framework, rules and regulations will suffice.[7]

Is the Malaysian government capable of this? No chance. It doesn't recognize that it has a problem. This is partly because it is shielded from the consequences of its "slapdash" approach by Petronas' oil revenues.

Cleaning up Corruption the Malaysian Way

Prime Minister Abdullah Badawi came to office in 2003 claiming that he would tackle corruption. To date, his has been one of the most ineffectual efforts imaginable. The man he appointed to head up the Anti-Corruption Agency was soon accused of corruption himself. At about the same time, a deputy police minister was accused of taking bribes to set criminal suspects free. The prime minister did not require either man to step aside while investigations were made. Instead, he insisted that 85% of corruption allegations proved baseless. But then that is because most are so inadequately investigated in the first place.[8]

Top-level impropriety is one thing, but the most fundamental component of Malaysia's system of law – the police – absolutely stinks with corruption. A survey by Transparency International found that the police were nominated by the public and by business as Malaysia's most corrupt institution, far ahead of, say, public works authorities or land offices. Sadly, many Malaysians simply assume that police are corrupt everywhere. A Royal Commission established by Abdullah called for an independent police complaints body to be set up. But the police chiefs objected, and so it was not set up.

Why are Malaysia's police so poor? It comes down to leadership. The minister with oversight of the police in Malaysia is the home affairs minister, and who was that before Abdullah Badawi was appointed prime minister? It was Abdullah himself. If he failed then to root out corruption among Malaysia's police, why should he do any better now?

Malaysia needs to lift its game. It needs to get its institutions right. A country this modern and relatively wealthy simply shouldn't have a police force this bad. There must be greater transparency too. But instead Malaysia is static. Malaysia has a lot of work to do. And with its oil due to run out, it will have less to do it with.

Suggestions for Business Strategists and Scenario Developers

▶ Investors in Malaysia should not count on the preferment policies that favor Malays being removed or substantially modified when they develop scenarios for Malaysia's future. Sound economic policy might call for their removal but Malaysia's electorate will not. And despite perceptions to the contrary, Malaysia does have a functioning democracy in which the government is acutely sensitive to the demands of the Malays.

▶ A significant risk to the Malaysian economy is the continued brain drain inherent in bright, young non-Malays (and even some Malays) who become discouraged by the lack of reform in Malaysia and simply leave for other economies where they can be treated the same as everyone else.

▶ A national ethos has developed in Malaysia whereby many like to delude themselves as to Malaysia's place in the world, which means that many have an exaggerated idea of how well Malaysia is doing. Unfortunately, this serves to lessen the consensus for reform at a time when Malaysia needs to do more just to keep up with other countries in the region. Underperformance in Malaysia often is not attributed to policy lethargy but blamed on outsiders. Self-delusion and xenophobia are risks in Malaysia in coming years.

Notes

1　The projection regarding net oil imports is from a briefing by Hassan Merican, Petronas' president and CEO, cited in *Business Times*, "Will M'sia get too reliant on Petronas for revenue?" June 29, 2007.

2　Reuters, November 14, 2006.

3　The arguments here draw on a column of mine published in *The Age*, under the heading "Whilst Malaysia fiddles, its opportunities are running dry," November 15, 2006. The column was widely distributed and debated in Malaysia, and drew criticism from Malaysia's trade minister, who dismissed it on the grounds that it was written by a "foreigner."

4　Asia Strategic Leadership Institute, "Corporate equity distribution: Past trends and future policy," 2006.

5　*Business Times*, "Will M'sia get too reliant on Petronas for revenue?" June 29, 2007.

6　*New Straits Times*, "More seeking to migrate since last month," December 19, 2006.

7　Tunku Abdul Aziz, "Iskandar Development Region – Lessons from Singapore and HK, *New Straits Times*, March 11, 2007.

8　*The Economist*, "Cleaning up?," March 24, 2007.

20 | China's Healthcare Sector to Boom

▷ China's population is ageing. Its healthcare system has fallen apart.

▷ But China is getting rich fast. And so hospitals and other healthcare facilities in China are set to be huge business in the coming decades.

▷ China's healthcare costs are on the verge of exploding. The Chinese government will look for preventive measures as well as curative ones for its population. Cigarettes and tobacco are a likely target. There is a chance that China might even consider banning cigarettes.

China's population is ageing and unhealthy. The one-child policy introduced in 1979 has led to this rapid ageing, giving China an age population profile that's getting close to that of a developed country. For example, the current median population age in China is 33.2 years. This is far in excess of India at 24.8 years, or even Turkey at 28.6 years. In fact, it's more akin to the US, where the population has a median age of 36.6 years.

More than 10% or around 140 million Chinese are classified as elderly. By 2030, that number will grow to 300 million. And by 2050, the UN's Population Division has forecast that the median age of China's population will be 45 years – more than the estimate for the US of 41 years and the UK at 42 years.[1] Such rapid ageing has huge implications for China's pension arrangements and healthcare costs.

People smoke everywhere in China. This is also contributing to the nation's health bill. So too is environmental pollution, particularly air quality. But is China's healthcare system ready for the coming onslaught? Anything but. It is in an extraordinary mess. It was never of a high order, but in rural areas healthcare delivery has largely collapsed and in urban areas it is beset by policy uncertainty and patchwork funding arrangements. It is in a state of transition but to what remains unclear. Its appalling state is extraordinary, given China's socialist pretensions. Indeed, the government-dominated health insurance schemes of countries like the UK and Australia are Marxist nirvanas in comparison.

What all this means is that healthcare is going to be a huge, booming sector in China in the coming decades, particularly with China's newfound wealth. Currently, healthcare accounts for just 3% of China's GDP. But in modern economies such as the US and Japan, the figure is more like 10%. So China has a lot of catching up to do. Indeed, spending on the sector won't just rise but accelerate. Spending on healthcare tends to grow faster than income as economies develop, and when populations age.

What is the government's response? It has no choice other than to liberalize its healthcare system to cope with the demands placed on it by wealthier, energized consumers who want more and a population that is ageing. And that is exactly what is happening – from primary healthcare, to hospitals, to health insurance.

A Neglected Discipline

The current mess has long antecedents. At no stage in its 5,000-year history did surgery become a significant part of Chinese traditional medicine and healthcare. The body was seen as an inviolable whole. Acupuncture was as invasive as healthcare generally got. Meanwhile, in Europe, doctors were experimenting with cadavers and eventually on live people to develop surgery – a whole new discipline of medicine.

Apart from Confucian restrictions on human vivisection, one theory as to why surgery did not take off in China is that circumcision was not practiced on account of Chinese males having small foreskins. And without this starting point, surgery had little to build on.

Eunuchs who were employed by the emperors as their palace servants, bureaucrats, and advisers – up to 70,000 at a time – present a counter-argument, however, through castration.

Access to the palace often meant influence and great wealth. Many eunuchs became rich through bribe taking and were able to afford their own mansions and country houses. Consequently, the demand to become a eunuch was very high.

But other than castration, surgery remained an undeveloped discipline in China. Even today there is still a preference for traditional healing. One reason might be the state of China's conventional healthcare system. China provided universal healthcare, although largely at a rudimentary level, before the market reforms of the 1980s. The system collapsed in the early 1980s as rural communes broke down and private enterprise became more important.

The long absence of market forces during the communist era has left hospitals moribund and crowded. There remains an almost total absence of conventional primary care: there are few independent doctors, or even neighborhood clinics, so people attend hospitals for almost every healthcare need.

The government is now experimenting in some urban areas with Community Health Service (CHS) clinics, which rely on government funding and co-payments from users. They are intended to provide primary healthcare to anyone. The co-payments can be high, however, and constitute the bulk of a medical bill.[2]

Hospital funding itself is complex and confused. The central, provincial, and local governments fund hospitals, and in the past, medical care was provided either at no or very little charge. The government has begun to explore ways to run its hospitals more efficiently. Some government-owned hospitals have been encouraged to convert to private ownership. Hospitals vary widely in competence and quality. Beijing, for example, has several specialist hospitals that are well equipped, but in many rural areas, hospitals have almost no modern equipment to speak of.

State-owned hospitals increasingly are being permitted to contract out some or all of their management. The municipal government of Suzhou, for example, issued tenders in 2005 for the management of most of its public hospitals while retaining ownership. Others are being permitted to partially privatize by accepting private capital. And in some regions such as Zhejiang-Jiangsu, foreigners have been allowed to invest directly in new hospitals. From the patients' perspective, the biggest change relates to cost. Rudimentary healthcare used to be free or almost free. But now anything more must be paid for.

Healthcare spending has grown hugely in China in recent years. Facilities have been upgraded and now, for those who have the money to spend, a better standard of healthcare can be purchased in China than ever before. Essentially, a user-pays situation now operates for diagnostic tests, drugs, and many kinds of treatment. Healthcare in China can be of a good standard – for those who can afford it. Those who work in solvent, larger state-owned enterprises, the government, and those in the private sector with employer-sponsored health cover generally do have affordable access to healthcare. The rest do not.

A basic employee medical insurance scheme has been introduced in urban areas but most still are not covered. This and spiraling healthcare costs in China have seen the private health insurance market rocket. That market is worth around US$5 billion and growing at 15–20% per annum. But there's still a long way to go. More than 130 million people now have private health cover but that means that around 90% do not. Obviously there is room for much more growth. One estimate is that by 2020, China's private health insurance market will have expanded fourteenfold to US$56 billion.[3]

But greater private health cover and the availability of better health services are leading to overservicing. One study estimated that around half of all babies born in Chinese hospitals are delivered by Caesarean section and in some hospitals the figure was as much as 70%. But before 1978, only 10% of births were by Caesarean. Cuts in government funding to hospitals have also seen hospitals and clinics push the sale of drugs as a means of raising additional cash.[4]

The pharmaceutical market is growing exponentially. Cash-hungry hospitals pushing drugs onto patients is one reason. But growing household incomes and of course ageing are also fuelling demand. The pharmaceutical industry is extremely regionalized and fractured. Some 7,500 local drug makers control 70% of the drug market but no one company controls more than 4%. And yet the market is estimated to be the world's fifth biggest by 2010.[5] There is plenty of scope for industry growth but also industry restructuring, with mergers, acquisitions, and national brand building. The industry is beset with faking and copyright fraud, however. Unlike India, there are few Chinese pharmaceutical companies that are well known for their ethics, quality control, and in a position to manufacture international quality drugs, but that will change.

In mid-2007, Zheng Xiaoyu, the former head of China's State Food and Drug Administration, was executed for taking bribes to approve drugs without the proper procedures having been followed. China's State Council ordered that the licenses for 170,000 drugs be reviewed to determine the circumstances of their approval.[6] China, it seemed, was intent on at least appearing to embark on a cleanup of its drug administration.

The market for medical equipment in China is also growing rapidly. It's now worth around US$13 billion annually. The China International Medical Equipment Fair held twice a year in Harbin is Asia's largest international medical equipment show. It opened to foreign exhibitors in 2004 and now attracts around 1,000 exhibitors from around the world. It has become an important means by which foreign medical equipment suppliers find agents and distributors in China.

Other ancillary services will grow exponentially too, with the prospects of foreign involvement. Managing medical waste in China is a niche market already worth around US$300 million annually, but this will grow as more hospitals are opened and more medical procedures are carried out. It includes appropriate handling and disposal of sharps, blood and blood products, body parts, chemicals, pharmaceuticals, radioactive materials, and medical devices. One Singapore company, United Engineers, is already involved in the business in China, with a presence in 10 Chinese cities, covering more than 100,000 hospital beds.[7]

Could China Ban Smoking?

China is the world's biggest market for tobacco, with more than 350 million smokers and more taking up the habit each day. It costs China billions. Three of the top four causes of death in China are smoking related: cerebral vascular disease, bronchitis and chronic pulmonary emphysema, liver cancer, and pneumonia. (Interestingly, the fifth biggest cause of death is suicide – on average, 287,000 suicides were recorded annually in recent years.)[8]

China's authorities are taking more interest in the adverse health effects and costs of cigarette smoking. The Ministry of Health estimated in 2007 that nearly one million Chinese die each year from smoking-related diseases, 100,000 die from diseases caused by passive smoking, and more than half a billion "suffer" from passive smoking.[9]

Clearly, banning smoking is an option if China wants to find one way to cut its health bill as its population ages more quickly than most Western countries. To date, it has banned smoking on public transport. The next step will be a ban on smoking in public places. A possible future step could be a ban on cigarette sales altogether.

Conventional wisdom is that so many Chinese smoke – it is so culturally ingrained – that China could never ban smoking. Certainly only one other country has banned the sale of tobacco products outright: Bhutan in 2004. But China banned having more than one child even though large families and having sons were part of the culture. Spitting in public was part of the culture too. But many of China's cities have banned that. Opium use was once widespread. So too was foot binding. Not now.

China's government is authoritarian and always has been. It has the power to effect monumental cultural change. And banning or severely curtailing tobacco and cigarettes would have an immediate and huge impact on public health. The Chinese state owns cigarette factories in China. But it also has to pick up much of the cost of public healthcare. It readily acknowledges the harmful health effects of smoking – it was a signatory to the WHO's 2003 Framework Convention on Tobacco Control, which commits countries to restricting how tobacco is sold, packaged, and advertised. The world's biggest tobacco companies are keen for access to the Chinese market. It is big and growing and so represents a potentially convenient replacement for the contracting markets of the West. But will this be borne out? It is unlikely that China will prove to be the long-term gold mine that the big tobacco companies believe it will be. A sudden seismic policy shift on smoking by the Chinese government is quite possible, particularly as ageing pressures push China's healthcare costs skywards. Other than smokers who want to keep smoking and the state-owned cigarette producers, the biggest losers will be tobacco growers. But they are concentrated in the southern Yunnan province. China is not a democracy and disquiet among them can be contained. Ageing is unavoidable. Smoking is not.

Boom Times Ahead

China as a consumer market will be big. But China as a healthcare market will be bigger. Most Chinese will get old before they get rich enough to buy many of the household goods that are the norm in the West.

China's current GDP in dollars is US$2.6 trillion. Assuming that GDP grows at 7% a year on average, then by 2030, China's GDP in 2007 dollars will be US$13.19 billion. Developed countries tend to spend around 10% of their GDP on healthcare. But assuming that, by 2030, China spends 8% of its GDP on the sector, then in 2030, China will be spending just over one trillion dollars a year in 2007 dollars on healthcare.

Suggestions for Business Strategists and Scenario Developers

▶ Healthcare in China has a very bright future – China is becoming wealthier very quickly, the current healthcare system is in a mess, and the population is ageing. The government needs to take action quickly.

▶ Currently, China spends relatively little of its GDP on healthcare, but in coming years expenditure can be expected to rise faster than economic growth. Increasingly, foreign involvement will be welcomed.

▶ Nursing homes are an anathema to many in Asia. But with the growing number of old, single men, there will be little option in coming decades other than to care for them in a nursing home or retirement village format. This may be a new area for investment in China in years to come.

▶ Health insurance will be a big market in years to come.

▶ Pharmaceuticals also has a big future. There are few national brands and the industry is ripe for dramatic restructuring.

▶ Hospitals will be big business in China. But so too will many ancillary services such as medical waste management.

▶ Western cigarette companies are likely to find that China will not prove to be the massive new market that they had hoped.

Notes

1   *The Economist*, "Staying young," July 16, 2005.
2   Heller, P., "Is Asia prepared for an aging population?," IMF Working Paper, WP/06/272, December, 2006.
3   *International Herald Tribune*, "Foreign health insurers seek clients in China," March 30, 2006.
4   *International Herald Tribune*, "Health care falls short, Chinese tell leaders," August 20, 2005.
5   *Business Times*, "Investors ignore scandals and chase Chinese drug firms," May 16, 2007.
6   *Financial Times*, "China sentences ex-drug official to death," May 29, 2007.
7   *Business Times*, "Medical waste management could be UE's net growth engine," May 30, 2007.
8   *People's Daily*, "Suicide, fifth biggest cause of death in China: Survey," November 29, 2002.
9   Reuters, "100,000 Chinese die annually from passive smoking," May 29, 2007.

21

The Next Tsunami: Mainland Chinese Tourists

▷ By 2020 or even by 2015, around 100 million tourists will pour out of mainland China every year.

▷ China will be the world's fourth biggest destination for tourists by 2010.

▷ China's own credit card, China Union Pay, is set to become a world-recognized brand, accepted in countries around the world.

▷ China will need to acquire more than 100 new passenger and freight aircraft *every* year for the next 20 years, worth some US$200 billion, and train thousands of pilots, so that in 2025, it will have around 55,000 pilots.

One of the most extraordinary demographic changes underway in Asia relates not to birth rates, longevity, or gender but simply to mobility. It wasn't long ago that most mainland Chinese effectively were banned from leaving China even if they had the means to travel. Now millions are temporarily outside China at any one time. And in years to come, millions more will be.

The Chinese government approved the first batch of outbound travel destinations in 1997, including Thailand, Singapore, the Philippines, Malaysia, Hong Kong, and Macau. In that year, 5.32 million trips were made. By 2002, the number had risen to 16.6 million. By 2004, it was 28.9 million. The number of mainland Chinese tourists traveling abroad has increased fiftyfold in the past 20 years and is growing at around 20% a year. The Economist Intelligence Unit has estimated that it will be 60 million by 2010 and 100 million by 2015. The WTO believes that the 100 million figure will be reached later – in 2020. In any event, the WTO estimates that China will be the world's biggest tourist destination by 2010 and the world's fourth biggest source of tourists.[1]

The list of approved destinations is now almost 100. In Europe, France is the most popular destination – around 700,000 mainland Chinese visited the country in 2005 – followed by Italy.[2] Possibly by 2015, Chinese will be either the first or second biggest national group to visit France each year, ahead of the British, Americans, and Japanese, according to the Paris Tourist Board.[3] The lure is not history, art, or food. It's shopping.

Indeed, it's not simply the numbers of mainlanders who now travel that makes the phenomenon so interesting, but how much they spend and on what. According to research by Goldman Sachs, they spend per capita at least what the Japanese now spend when they travel abroad.[4] It's a surprising result, given the vastly different per capita GDPs of the two economies.

Mainland travelers prefer to stay in middle-range hotels and spend relatively little on food, leaving perhaps 50–70% of their total holiday budget for shopping. This contrasts with typical Western travelers, who prefer to spend more on accommodation and services. Acquiring "trophies" from their trip abroad is important to many mainland Chinese. They like to buy luxury goods that can be shown off to the people back home. Also, gift giving is important. It builds "face" for both the giver and the receiver, so items need to be acquired, not just for one or two people but often for a wide circle of relatives, friends, and work colleagues.

But the preference for luxury goods does not mean that the mainlanders are indifferent to price: they want branded goods but want to pay as little for them as possible. Luxury goods tend to be 20–30% cheaper in Europe or Hong Kong compared with China, due to high tariffs and consumption taxes there. They tend to take a long time to make their purchasing decisions, comparing prices and being sensitive to even the smallest differences.

What do mainland Chinese like to see when they are abroad? Other than obvious tourist attractions that are a must so that they can be photographed in front of them to show friends and relatives back home, department stores are popular itinerary stops. Also, mainland Chinese like to visit the local Chinatown, be they in Kuala Lumpur, Paris, or London. They are curious to see how other Chinese live around the world. Red-light districts are popular with male Chinese, and casinos are popular with both sexes.

China Union Pay, China's own credit card that was set up in 2002, is increasingly being accepted outside China, with the rapid rise of the mainland Chinese tourist. Many major Paris department stores now accept it.

Some automatic cash machines in Australia, the US, Egypt, and Germany accept the cards. The card is set for phenomenal growth around the world as countries and retailers rush to accept it. It is likely to be one of the best known Chinese brands outside China within a decade, its logo joining those of Visa and MasterCard at cash machines and tills around the world.

Mainland Chinese are new travelers to foreign countries. And so many behave in ways that locals find unpleasant. A mainland group might, for example, be traveling on a day boat trip on pristine Swedish lakes, only to start throwing their used soft drink cans and empty cigarette packets into the lake from the boat. Or they might pile into an Italian church, talking loudly, and using their flash bulbs during a service. This sort of behavior led the Chinese government in 2006 to consider passing legislation to ban or restrict from overseas travel those citizens who have shown themselves to be repeat offenders at this sort of thing. There is also a huge problem of inbound tourists carving their names or messages into trees and onto walls in favorite holiday spots around China. The Chinese government is concerned that inappropriate behavior on the part of its citizens when they travel may harm China's image internationally.[5]

Mainlanders Head to the Rest of Asia

Asian destinations account for around 90% of the overseas travel by mainlanders at present. Southeast Asia is the most popular destination. It is not too far and relatively inexpensive. Plus Mandarin can be spoken widely and Chinese food is readily available.

China was once spurned by the governments of Southeast Asia. They were fearful of the spread of communism via ethnic Chinese networks. For example, Malaysians were simply banned from visiting mainland China. Anything printed with Chinese characters was banned in Indonesia as were Chinese-language schools. Printed Chinese matter was even a prohibited import and customs forms given to all travelers required that Chinese literature and Chinese medicines be declared along with narcotics, firearms, and pornography. It's a different story today. Mainland Chinese do not bring communism with them when they travel. They bring cash.

Singapore is among the Southeast Asian destinations desperate to make itself attractive to mainland Chinese tourists but oddly, given its "clean" image, it seems intent on courting the seedier side of international tourism. Approval has been given for two mega casinos, known locally as "integrated resorts" (the local media has been instructed not to refer to them as casinos), particularly aimed at attracting mainland Chinese and Indonesian gamblers. A consortium headed by Las Vegas Sands will build and operate the first casino – a US$3.6 billion hotel, gaming, and convention center complex due to open in 2009. The government also allowed a local franchise of the Paris Crazy Horse nude review to open but it closed after a year's operation. And it allows brothels to operate openly in as many as six designated red-light areas (DRAs). Many of the women who work in the brothels are from mainland China, this being seen as a plus for attracting mainland tourists. Singapore also has established direct air routes to secondary Chinese cities, allowing it to more easily attract visitors from across China rather than simply Shanghai and Beijing.

Indonesia too has relaxed the ban on Chinese literature – tourism brochures can now be printed in Chinese. Plus, the teaching of Chinese is no longer banned so that Indonesians can now train to be tour guides for mainland Chinese tour groups. However, Indonesia still suffers from the immense stigma that arose during the rioting in Jakarta in 1998, in which the shophouses of local Chinese were looted and destroyed and many local Chinese women were raped either by sections of the military or at their behest. Many Chinese from outside Indonesia refuse to travel there as a matter of principal.

Half of Hong Kong's visitors now come from mainland China. In 2006, they accounted for around 12 million of the estimated 25 million visitors to the territory, whereas in 2001, they made up less than a third of the 13.7 million visitors. By the end of 2006, Hong Kong had almost 45,000 hotel rooms in 123 hotels and a further 5,400 rooms provided by almost 500 guest houses. Hotels owned by mainland Chinese companies have been among the newer hotels to have opened.

Hong Kong is continuing to open new attractions and upgrade existing ones. The Hong Kong Wetland Park opened in May 2006 and Hong Kong Disneyland opened the previous September. The Disneyland franchise has been modified to make it more appealing to mainland Chinese tourists. For example, advertising showing the venue as a place for families has been amended to show parents with only one child, as most mainland families have only one child on account of China's one-child policy.

Australia has become an important destination too. It was accredited as a tourist destination by the Chinese government in 1999. The number of mainland Chinese arriving as short-term visitors to Australia has increased by more than 20% each year since then so that by 2007 one in 15 short-term visitors was a mainland Chinese. China was the fifth most important source of short-term visitors to Australia, behind New Zealand, the UK and Japan. It is likely to be the third most important source by 2009 and the second biggest by 2012.[6]

Visitors to China

The corollary to the millions of Chinese who are pouring out of China is the tourist trade to China. The WTO estimates that by 2020, foreigners visiting China will reach 210 million annually, and tourism will account for more than US$300 billion or 8–11% of China's GDP.[7] The 2008 Beijing Olympics and the 2010 World Expo in Shanghai will provide big boosts to visitor numbers and, even more importantly, to China's image abroad as a well-developed and relatively comfortable tourist destination.

Statistics on visitors to China need to be treated with caution, however. For example, in 2006, 124 million visits to mainland China were recorded but 74 million of these were by Hong Kong residents. Another 22 million were Macau residents. Only 22 million were by actual foreigners. But what this does mean is that the WTO estimates expect that by 2020, 10 times the current number of foreigners will visit China annually. Also, most of the 124 million were day visitors; they did not stay overnight. Of the foreigners, 1.7 million were from the US and 5.3 million from Europe. About half the foreign visits were holiday related. The rest were a mixture of business travel, visits by people as part of a crew, or visits to see relatives.[8] The Chinese government has estimated that visitors to mainland China spent US$29.3 billion in 2005 for example.

The government estimates that tourism directly employs more than six million Chinese, with 500,000 being added every year. The sector has been opened to foreign investment in line with WTO requirements. Indeed, the China National Tourism Administration agreed in 2003 to allow the first 100% foreign-owned travel service to set up – four years ahead of the schedule as determined by China's WTO agreements.

After a poor start, China's commercial airline industry is developing a good reputation. The airlines have well-maintained new fleets and China is building many new, well-designed airports. The safety record is much improved. A series of crashes saw the government act swiftly to restructure the sector and improve its regulation.

China's big three airlines, Air China, China Eastern, and China Southern, are all partially listed overseas. (They were required to absorb seven regional airlines in 2002.) And the Civil Aviation Administration of China has developed a reputation for being conservative and cautious in recent years. Budget airlines are being established but one obstacle is that few Chinese cities have secondary (and thus cheaper) airports. This has been an important ingredient for the budget airline industry elsewhere.

China's airline industry, already experiencing exponential growth (passenger numbers have been growing at 30–40% annually), is set to grow even faster. In 2005, there were around 11,000 pilots employed to fly around 800 commercial aircraft in China.[9] Boeing estimated that China would need more than 2,400 new passenger and freight aircraft worth almost US$200 billion by 2025, by which time around 55,000 pilots would be required. Such an incredible increase is possible. China is upgrading its airports, building new ones, and extending runways. The contrast with India could barely be starker.

Suggestions for Business Strategists and Scenario Developers

▶ Catering to mainland Chinese tourists has quickly become a significant business. But it will become much bigger in coming decades. Mostly, they prefer to stay in business-class hotels rather than first-class hotels, so more demand for hotels in the middle price range can be expected worldwide but particularly in Southeast Asia, France, Italy, and the UK.

▶ Governments, state and regional, in mainland China will do well to advertise their localities as tourist destinations, having taken due care to research what mainland Chinese find attractive in a destination. Many might consider opening tourism offices in China, not just in Shanghai and Beijing but perhaps in other centers such as Chengdu and Shenzhen.

▶ The world's aircraft manufacturers already know that China will be a massive market in coming years for jet aircraft. But there are plenty of ancillary services associated with this sector that are also set to boom in coming decades, such as improved reservations systems, inflight catering provision, administering flight reward programs, pilot training, inflight magazine provision and associated language translation, inflight entertainment provision, possibly including gaming, and aircraft maintenance.

Notes

1   *Asia Times*, "China's tourism gives as much as it takes," April 13, 2005.
2   *New York Times*, "Chinese speak the international language of shopping," November 7, 2006.
3   Op. cit. *Asia Times*, April 13, 2005.
4   *Asia Times*, "Outbound tourism sector on rise in China," October, 2006.
5   *Asia Times*, "Chinese travelers' uncivil liberties," October, 2006.
6   *The Age*, "Chinese tourist numbers set to top Japan," June 19, 2007.
7   Op. cit. *Asia Times*, April 13, 2005.
8   Figures are from the China National Tourist Office.
9   *International Herald Tribune*, "China's lack of pilots slows aviation growth," June 27, 2005.

Medical Research to Shift to Asia

▷ Animal rights activists are making it difficult to perform laboratory testing on animals in the West. But animal testing will not go away. It will simply shift to Asia, particularly China and Singapore where authoritarian governments keep activist groups under control and constrain debate in the media.

▷ Other types of research such as stem cell research, which also generates ethical concerns in the West, is shifting to Asia, for similar reasons.

Medical research is facing a crisis in the West. Ethical, religious, and moral concerns are hampering research like never before. Scientists face attack from politicians, the media, pressure groups, and religious bodies. Such attacks are the inevitable result of Western, plural liberalism that allows for everyone to be given a voice. And so stem cell research, for example, has been under threat in the US and animal testing is threatened in every Western country, most vociferously in the UK. So what can scientists and big drug companies do? The answer is that they can shift their research and testing to countries that are not plural liberal democracies, and where pressure groups have little voice and the media is muzzled; essentially to where authoritarian governments ride roughshod over ethical and moral concerns – countries like China and Singapore. In fact, virtually every major Asian government is now attempting to develop a local life sciences industry using a combination of tax and other incentives.

And so in the coming decades, it is likely that many of the world's medical experiments and testing will be conducted under the auspices of Asia's dictatorial governments. It seems that authoritarianism sometimes does pay financial dividends. Some of Asia's governments are actually making a virtue of their authoritarianism, as they seek to promote themselves as secure destinations for medical research and animal testing.

It's not just drug companies that benefit from Asia's autocrats. Monsanto, Delta, and Pine Land have all planted genetically modified (GM) cotton in China. Once their products are approved in China, the relative absence of environmental and consumer groups that are focused on GM crops make the activities of such companies easier. They can get on with business rather than fight media campaigns and legal battles. By 2006, China already had 3.3 million hectares under GM cotton production – an area roughly the size of Belgium. Chinese scientists were also experimenting with GM cabbages, corn, melons, papaya, peanuts, potatoes, soybeans, tomatoes, wheat, and tobacco. And the Chinese government was spending more than US$100 million annually on biotech crop research – more than any other government other than the US. A constrained media also makes for ignorant, and so more passive, consumers. One study of 1,000 consumers conducted in 12 supermarkets in Beijing found that 65% of those surveyed were not "acquainted" with the concept of GM products.[1]

Cost is a big factor too but then that's linked to legal costs. India is among the countries with an emerging biotech industry. Wages for researchers are relatively low in India and there are fewer legal complications than in, say, the US. Bristol-Myers of the US is one company to have set up research facilities in India. In 2007, it announced that it would expand its research facilities in Bangalore to accommodate as many as 400 scientists.[2]

Another reason to set up in Asia is to curry favor with local governments. The Swiss pharmaceutical giant Novartis announced in 2006 its intention to build a US$100 million research facility in Shanghai that would one day accommodate as many as 400 "mainly" Chinese scientists. Such a facility will help Novartis to tailor its products for the Chinese and other Asian markets, but it was almost certainly also part of the company's strategy to improve relations with the Chinese government for when it decides in the future what medicines to buy for its citizens.[3]

Animal Testing

A farm in Staffordshire, UK that had bred guinea pigs for medical research for more than 30 years stopped doing so at the end of 2005 after the family that owned it and others connected to the business had been subjected to a six-year campaign of abuse and intimidation by animal rights extremists. The family and those connected with them had been subjected to death threats, hate mail, malicious phone calls, hoax bombs, and arson attacks. Suppliers were similarly targeted: one was hit by a brick thrown through a window and subjected to an anonymous campaign that he was a pedophile. The abuse reached a crescendo in 2005 when the remains of the mother-in-law of a part-owner of the farm were dug up from a nearby churchyard and stolen.[4] It was the last straw for the farm's owners. They announced that they would cease breeding guinea pigs for research by the end of the year. The animal rights extremists were handed another victory and research guinea pigs would now be even more expensive in the UK.

It has been estimated that 10–15% of the costs of drug discovery in the US and the UK goes toward animal testing.[5] And that the total cost of bringing a new drug to the market is in excess of US$1 billion. Thus, the pharmaceutical industry needs to find ways to cut costs.

China supplies most of the world's primates used in animal testing. But a monkey used in China in preclinical testing costs about one-fifth of the US$5,000 that US researchers typically must pay for a monkey sourced from within the US.[6]

Nor is there much organized concern for animal rights and welfare in China. Indeed, concern for animal welfare is given a low priority even in basic animal husbandry.

Increasingly, Western drug companies and others that use own testing will relocate such testing to China. Some will relocate their testing facilities to China. But already animal testing outsourcing companies are starting up in China.

The US firm Bridge Pharmaceuticals (which was spun off from the Stanford Research Institute in 2004) opened an animal testing joint venture, Vital Bridge Zhongguancun Drug Development Laboratory, in November 2005 in the Zhongguancun Life Sciences Park in a northern Beijing suburb.[7] The facility is the first US Food and Drug Administration (FDA) and SFDA (China's FDA equivalent) compliant preclinical laboratory in China. The laboratory acts as a contract animal testing facility on behalf of client firms such as drug and cosmetic companies. It can reduce animal testing costs by more than 50% on US costs. It claims to observe US regulations with regard to animal care and use, although it must be said that regulatory enforcement in China is far less reliable than in the US. Also, other checks and balances such as those imposed by the media, pressure groups, and opposition politicians barely exist in China.

Locally owned, Shanghai-based WuXi PharmaTech is another company in China that's now in the outsourcing animal testing market. It offers global pharmaceutical/biopharmaceutical companies diverse outsourcing services, including outsourced animal testing that it has offered since 2005. By 2007, it claimed 19 of the world's top 20 pharmaceutical companies as its customers and 8 of the top 10 biopharmaceutical companies.

Singapore has been particularly aggressive in attracting biotech scientists from around the world in its efforts to develop its own biotech sector. Philip Yeo, the then chairman of Singapore's Agency for Science, Technology and Research, said at the time of his drive to recruit top scientists in the field from around the world that:

> I promise them secure funding for their research, reasonable time horizons, the best facilities I can afford and enough mice for their research.[8]

That last remark was particularly important. It was a signal to researchers in the UK and the US that they could expect to work in Singapore with research animals and not face the protests and harassment they face elsewhere as they go about their work. Singapore's Biopolis, a US$300 million research park that houses Singapore's fledging biotech sector, includes three levels of underground laboratories and room to house 150,000 research mice. Said Yeo:

> Try to get animal facilities in a place like the United Kingdom and be careful they don't burn your car.

The freedom from harassment from animal rights activists and a prying inquisitive media, plus huge tax incentives and upfront cash incentives, has attracted several leading researchers to Singapore. Debate in Singapore is strictly controlled as is all the country's media. Public debate over the ethics of animal testing is unlikely to get started in Singapore unless the government sanctions it. Indeed, public debate over anything serious is rarely permitted in Singapore.

Research institutions in Singapore have had to follow new, standardized guidelines on the use and care of research animals since November 2004. Prior to that, there were no national guidelines. Violations of the guidelines can result in up to a year in prison and a fine of up to S$10,000 (US$5,900). Jail sentences are unlikely. The maximum fine is simply the price of one research monkey in the US.

Stem Cell Research and Authoritarianism

Stem cells grow into various tissues and theoretically at least could be used to replace dying cells in the brain, heart, and other organs. In this way, stem cell procedures might provide treatment for degenerative ailments such as Alzheimer's disease. The ethical problem comes from the fact that the cells are obtained from human embryos that are destroyed in the process.

But in the US, researchers have been hamstrung by the Bush administration's restrictions on federal funding for such research. And a separate US$3 billion stem cell initiative by the state government of California has been hampered by legal challenges.

Accordingly, scientists in the UK have made significant progress in stem cell research. The UK announced in late 2005 a doubling of existing financial commitments to stem cell research. And in Asia, scientists have been active in the field too, most particularly in South Korea, China, and Singapore where they do not face the moral and ethical barriers that are faced in the West.

The main centers for stem cell research in China are the Health Science Center at the Shanghai Institute of Biological Science, the Stem Cell Research Center at Peking University, HuaZhong University of Science and Technology in Wuhan, and the Shanghai Second Medical University.

South Korea too has been prominent in cloning and stem cell research. In October 2005, the World Stem Cell Hub was opened in Seoul in the presence of local, American, and British scientists. It aims to supply overseas labs with cloned embryonic stem cells. A setback occurred in late 2005 when Korea's most renowned stem cell researcher was forced to apologize for obtaining human eggs unethically. Unfortunately, the questioning of the scientist's methods did not originate in South Korea but in a foreign journal and from an American colleague.

Cashing in on a Lack of Liberalism: The Case of Singapore

The Singapore government actively encourages stem cell research. It also was the first government worldwide to allow cloned embryos to be kept for up to 14 days, something which few other governments have been prepared to allow. As one newspaper commented:

> You can't buy Wrigley's Spearmint Chewing gum in Singapore. But human embryonic stem cells? That's a different matter.[9]

While embryonic stem cell research remained severely constrained in the US, Singapore company ES Cell in 2006 became the first to produce human embryonic stem cells to be used in clinical tests commercially. It made them available online. Says its website:

> There is an upfront transfer fee of US$6,000 per cell line to cover associated production costs (does not include shipping).

In 1999, the government of Singapore nominated life sciences (medicine, pharmaceuticals, and biotechnology) as one of the country's four industrial "pillars" and in 2003, it announced that it would set aside around S$3 billion (US$1.7 billion) for the development of biomedical sciences in Singapore over the next five years. The country's Economic Development Board at that point estimated that biotechnology would account for around 10% of the country's manufacturing output by 2010. (It accounted for US$15.8 billion or 8.3% of the country's manufacturing output in 2004.)[10] And then in 2005, the government again raised its existing spending commitments on biotechnology to S$12 billion (US$7 billion) for the next five years.

It has since been shopping for the best experts that money can buy. Alan Coleman, the head of the team of researchers that cloned Dolly the sheep in Scotland, was an early recruit. He is the CEO of ES Cell International, a company largely owned by a venture capital fund established by Singapore's Economic Development Board. Edison Liu, a leading researcher at America's National Cancer Institute, was appointed head of Singapore's own Genome Institute. And Yoshiaki Ito and his research team were poached from Kyoto University to join Singapore's Institute of Molecular and Cell Biology.[11] Most local researchers in Singapore occupy relatively junior posts on research teams that generally are headed by expatriate talent from the US and elsewhere.

Novartis, GlaxoSmithKline, Schering Plough, and Eli-Lilly are among the multinational drug companies with production plants in Singapore that have also opened research facilities there. GlaxoSmithKline announced plans in November 2005 to build a S$115 million state-of-the-art R&D plant in Singapore. The plant will incorporate remote real-time monitoring, meaning that the company's experts will not even need to be in Singapore but can monitor results from Europe or the US.

Such remote real-time monitoring opens the way for experiments to be conducted in countries with lax regulations by scientists in countries where ethical and regulatory constraints hamper such experiments.

Singapore lacks a major drug or life sciences company of its own, but local start-ups have begun to appear. A Singapore biotech company, Cell-

Research Corporation, announced in July 2005 that it had found a new source of stem cells, from the umbilical cord lining.[12]

Local Singapore life sciences firm Lynk Biotechnologies has developed various creams that allow drugs to be absorbed through the skin. The company's plant includes animal testing facilities.[13] And scientists from Singapore's Institute of Bioengineering and Nanotechnology together with Japanese researchers announced their development of a new injectable hydrogel in December 2005 that would be suitable in cancer therapy as a means of delivering drugs to targeted sites. The gel, the researchers said, has already been tested on animals.[14]

One potential problem with Singapore's push to be a biomedical research center is that with a population of around four million, the scope for conducting large, regular clinical trials is reduced. But then Singapore is a transport hub and millions more people can be readily reached within a few hours. Not only that, but many of those potential candidates for clinical trials live in jurisdictions where legal protection is weak or where there is not a strong compensation culture as with, say, the US, ensuring that should something go wrong, their legal recourse is limited, thus reducing costs and potential costs for researchers based in Singapore.

And so trials such as those carried out in 2006 at Vietnam's National Hospital of Traditional Medicine by Singapore's CellResearch, in which allogeneic cord lining stem cell transplants were trialed to see how they affected wound healing without the need for a skin graft, will be more common in future.[15]

Keeping Labs Away from the West's Plural Democracies

Asia is where those activities shift that are too dirty or mundane to be done in rich, democratic countries. In the case of manufacturing, for example, the West's appropriate but costly antipollution laws have encouraged production to shift to China, where effluent is dumped into the air and waterways with little or no charge. And in the case of life sciences, testing on animals can be done in Asia, where it is cheaper, laws are less likely to be enforced if they exist at all, and queasy pressure groups are kept under the thumb.

Technological advances such as remote monitoring are improving all the time, hastening the shift to Asia. Within a few decades, most of the world's animal testing probably will be done in Asia. The West's animal rights activists will have succeeded not in closing down the industry but in chasing it away to where it is obscured from the prying eyes of regulators and the media and under the protective wing of Asia's autocratic governments.

Suggestions for Business Strategists and Scenario Developers

▶ Western universities, pharmaceutical and cosmetics companies that have not already considered contracting animal testing to Asia might consider doing so. The sector is an emerging one for Asia and likely to grow in importance.

▶ China will be a huge market for pharmaceuticals, so establishing research facilities in China is one way for foreign pharmaceutical companies to better position themselves for entering the Chinese market.

Notes

1 *International Herald Tribune*, "A battle for hearts and mouths," April 1–2, 2006.
2 *Business Times*, "India growing as biotech hub," April 12, 2007.
3 *International Herald Tribune*, "Novartis plans lab in Shanghai," November 6, 2006.
4 BBC News, "Targeted guinea pig farm closes," August 23, 2005.
5 *Red Herring*, "Bridge tests drugs in China," November 28, 2005.
6 *San Francisco Business Times*, "Building a bridge to bio-outsourcing," November 7, 2005.
7 Op. cit. *Red Herring*, November 28, 2005.
8 Pacific Bridge Medical, *Asian Medical Newsletter*, "Singapore: A prime location for biotechnology companies," **2**(11), February 4, 2003.
9 *International Herald Tribune*, "Singapore filling void in stem-cell research, with US 'help,'" August 17, 2006.
10 *International Herald Tribune*, "Singapore's biotechnology push," September 19, 2005.
11 *The Economist*, "Send in the clones," August 22, 2002.
12 Channel NewsAsia, "Singapore biotech firm discovers new source of stem cells," July 4, 2005.
13 *Straits Times*, "Life sciences firm Lynk gets $6m shot in the arm," July 4, 2005.
14 *Business Times*, "Singapore, Japan develop new medical gel," December 8, 2005.
15 *Business Times*, "CellResearch in talks with cord blood bank," April 5, 2006.

23

New Switzerlands: Private Banking and Money Laundering Shift to Asia

▷ Millionaires are being created all over Asia, including around 300,000 in China alone.

▷ China's fund management industry is likely to be worth US$1.4 trillion in 2016.

▷ Singapore is set to become a world center for private banking and hidden offshore funds.

Private banking is a relatively new phenomenon in Asia. It's now one of the region's newest, fastest growing service industries. Secret offshore banking, its shadier cousin, is growing too and Singapore particularly is making a pitch for this business. In years to come, Singapore is likely to become the new Switzerland, much to the consternation of other governments. China, on the other hand, will be one of the world's biggest markets for private banking and fund management.

China: Exploding Private Wealth

China now has around 300,000 US dollar millionaires. The wealthiest 5% of the population is believed to account for around half of all bank deposits.[1] And more than US$1.5 trillion in personal savings currently sit in Chinese bank accounts where they earn negligible interest.

New options are becoming available. Mutual funds have already made big inroads. Already, there are many hundreds of mutual funds based in

China. China will soon have the world's fastest growing funds industry. One study estimates that managed assets in China will grow 25% a year, swelling from around US$156 billion in 2007 to US$1.4 trillion by 2016, by which time fund managers can collectively expect to earn management fees in the vicinity of US$2–3 billion annually.[2]

Other options are being developed. Foreign banks have been permitted to open yuan-denominated banking services to domestic Chinese clients since December 1, 2006. As that date neared, foreign banks prepared more than 100 financial products and services to market in China, three times the number of financial products available from local banks.[3] Looser curbs on cross-border investment will see even more avenues for China's massive savings pool.

Regulatory conditions on wealth management services remain strict in China, however. Quite simply, developing and marketing financial products to individuals with, say, US$500,000 or more to invest seems anomalous in a country that is still ostensibly communist. Inevitably, the regulations will change simply because China needs to compete with what institutions can offer offshore. There's no point China's authorities denying that China now has an astounding number of rich people. The government is well aware of this from its own banking statistics.

Already perhaps 80% of the profits that even the local banks make come from local high net worth customers. The China Banking Regulatory Commission estimated that assets under management by onshore institutions will rise from US$910 billion in 2004 to US$1.73 trillion in 2009.[4]

India is another likely source of private banking demand. Wealth is being created in India like never before. But by international standards, local banks are very backward in what they have traditionally offered. But the Indian government is removing some restrictions. In early 2007, for example, it lifted the requirement that banks invest at least 25% of their deposits in public debt and other low-risk, low-yield securities. The thinking behind this requirement had been that it made the banking system more stable and less prone to banking runs, plus it provided the government with a big source of cheap financing for its own budget deficits. The state also owns around 70% of India's banking system. Bureaucrats do not make for an innovative, dynamic financial system and so, again, the sector is more sluggish and insensitive to customers' needs than it should be. Foreign exchange controls have also hampered the sector's development and so, overall, India's major banks are surprisingly small. They are many times smaller than China's, for example.

Wealthy Singapore Residents Lead the Way

Singapore has become the regional leader when it comes to private banking and financial innovation. No longer do wealthy Singaporeans need to send their money offshore. Citigroup, Credit Suisse, UBS, and Merrill Lynch are among the private banks with offices in Singapore employing many hundreds of staff. The Credit Suisse branch, for example, is as big in terms of staff as its London branch, the two only being exceeded by the Zurich office.

A critical mass of sufficiently rich locals, rich residents in neighboring countries keen to use Singapore's banks to hide their wealth, and a regulatory system that leads the region have all contributed.

In their first *Asia-Pacific Wealth Report*, Merrill Lynch and Capgemini concluded that at the end of 2005, Singapore was home to an estimated 55,000 high net worth individuals, 13.4% more than a year earlier. (High net worth individuals were defined as individuals holding more than US$1 million in net financial assets excluding their primary residence.) Singapore was also shown to have the highest number of high net worth individuals per capita among the eight Asian nations included in the study. Collectively, Singapore's high net worth individuals held US$260 billion in financial and investment assets. A third, or 18,000, were of Indonesian origin. Collectively, they accounted for US$87 billion of the assets.

The report went on to identify 700 individuals as ultra high net worth individuals with more than US$30 million in net financial assets. But among the eight Asian countries, the average net wealth of US$4.7 million was not the highest. Hong Kong's high net worth individuals had that honor with US$5.3 million, and then mainland China with US$5 million. The report also estimated that the financial wealth of the high net worth individuals in all the Asia Pacific region would grow at 6.7% to 2010 to reach US$10.6 trillion.

Singaporean investors were found to have the most varied portfolios, perhaps reflecting the wide range of investment options available to them. They had the highest allocation (37%) in the Asia Pacific region to investments such as hedge funds, managed funds, foreign currency, commodities, private equity, and fine art as opposed to mere cash and conventional bank deposits.

Singapore: The Emerging Switzerland

No longer do banks in Switzerland, Luxembourg, and Liechtenstein operate with complete secrecy, particularly since the introduction of the US Patriot

Act of 2001 in the wake of the September 11, 2001 terrorist attacks in the US. Their governments have faced great pressure from the EU and the US to exchange information on account holders. Plus, a 15% withholding tax was required to be applied on interest earned on accounts held by EU citizens from 2005, rising to 20% in 2008 and 35% in 2011. So Europe's private banking capitals are losing some of their attractiveness.

Enter Singapore. Singapore is good at making money. It is good at identifying a niche and then devoting considerable state resources to exploiting it, unhampered by local pressure groups, a troublesome opposition, or an inquisitive media. Thus Singapore has promoted itself as a haven for those who prefer banking secrecy. Nor does it levy any withholding tax on interest earned by nonresidents. Plus, as mentioned, it has an excellent banking regulatory regime and legal system, giving foreigners assurance that their money will be safe. Ample professional staff and excellent communications further assure foreigners.

Liechtenstein's LGT Bank was one of the first foreign private banking concerns to open in Singapore, doing so in 2003. Owned by Liechtenstein's royal family, one of its reasons for opening a Singapore office was to serve European clients looking to escape withholding tax. It could direct them to Singapore, with its less intrusive banking environment. EFG Private Bank of Switzerland, owned by the Greek Latsis family, was also granted an early license. It wanted to set up in Singapore for similar reasons.

Singapore is developing Islamic banking services to complement its existing range of services. Its neighbor Malaysia had a head start on this but Singapore's overwhelming technical and regulatory superiority will see it well placed to capture a good part of this market, not just from the region's 700 million or so Muslims but from the Middle East as well.

By 2006, it was thought that at least US$200 billion in private banking assets was being managed in Singapore.[5] That was just a small fraction of the funds being managed in Switzerland but shows how much room Singapore has for growth.

Any Money Will Do

For years, Singapore was reluctant to sign an extradition treaty with Indonesia and only agreed to do so in 2007. Up until then, many Indonesians wanted for corporate crimes in Indonesia only had to take the hour flight from Jakarta to Singapore to be out of reach of Indonesian law. What they brought with them was their money – lots of it. Hence the government's reluctance to sign an extradition treaty.

Singaporean officials make all the right noises when it comes to monitoring illicit funds. But there is a perception that, in practice, Singapore is not fully meeting international expectations and obligations. In the course of my research, one US official involved in monitoring international money flows described Singapore's efforts to date as "very disappointing." And a senior fund manager in the region had this to say to me:

> Singapore has truly become the global center for parking ill-gotten gains. The private banking teams are huge and in practice ask almost no questions (as compared to the branches elsewhere including Switzerland). An acquaintance of mine who made US$13 million through a corrupt deal [in Indonesia] was not asked anything about how he got the money, despite obviously having a job that would not have allowed such amounts to have been accumulated. Russians, mainland Chinese, and Indonesians are pouring money into Singapore. High-end property has risen 30–50% in the last 18 months or so.

Singapore, he argued, is out of step internationally. He cited a case in which even a Swiss bank cooperated with the Indonesian government in tracking down US$5.2 million in allegedly improper funds deposited by the former head of Bank Mandiri, Indonesia's largest state-owned bank. Be this as it may, it augers well for Singapore's development as a global private banking center.

Attention is now being turned to China, almost certainly the world's biggest source of ill-gotten proceeds in need of an offshore home. Singapore is working hard at making itself more attractive to Chinese mainlanders, be they tourists or individuals with funds to park. Singaporean government representatives are trawling through China, promoting Singapore over Hong Kong as a safe destination for funds and property investment. Direct flights are being established with regional centers across China. Casinos are being set up. There's even been an influx of mainland Chinese prostitutes into Singapore's quasi-legal sex industry. And there's no extradition treaty or little chance of one. Singapore will be the obvious home for money from mainland China in need of a safe home, particularly as trust is lost in Hong Kong and it is not seen as sufficiently distant from mainland China's authorities. Money from Vietnam and Myanmar too will flow in, to accompany the billions already there from Malaysia, Indonesia, and the Philippines. Ethnic Chinese links across all these economies will help to guarantee the cash flow. Singapore stands to gain billions. Its private banking sector will be massive in decades to come.

Suggestions for Business Strategists and Scenario Developers

▶ Fund management and private banking are set for astronomic growth in Asia.

▶ To attract a greater slice of the market, the region's governments will come under competitive pressure to improve their banking regulations and enforce these regulations in a clear and transparent manner.

▶ Singapore is emerging as a prominent international banking center that will serve not just Asia but Europe and the rest of the world in coming decades. The major threat will come from Western governments such as the US, which will press it to make greater disclosures about who holds what funds in Singapore and to collect more information on depositors.

Notes

1   International Herald Tribune, "Private bankers view China's new wealthy as rich prize," May 24, 2006.
2   The study, prepared by McKinsey & Co, is cited in Business Times, "Fund assets seen topping US$1.4t by 2016," March 16, 2007.
3   Op. cit. International Herald Tribune, May 24, 2006.
4   Op. cit. International Herald Tribune, May 24, 2006.
5   The Economist, "A new treasure island," August 19, 2006.

24

Asia's Coming Medical Tourism Bonanza

▷ Forty million Americans do not have health insurance or are underinsured. And many procedures are not covered by Europe's healthcare schemes.

▷ Asia has a solution: fly to its hospitals and have the surgery done there.

▷ Surgery is cheap. Partly because Asia's surgeons don't need to carry the malpractice insurance that US doctors do. And that's because legal systems in Asia are typically so poor that suing isn't an option.

Medical tourism is going to be big business in Asia. Already, it's a sector that's growing exponentially. The initial fillip for treating foreigners has come from the large communities of Western expatriates already in Asia, particularly Southeast Asia. They and their families gave Southeast Asia's better hospitals plenty of exposure to treating educated, more demanding, and wealthier patients. Tourism too has been important. Plenty of Western tourists, usually with health insurance cover at least for the duration of their vacation, injure themselves or fall ill during their stays in Thailand, for example. It is not a big leap to then offer medical services to non-resident foreigners who travel for the specific reason of accessing those services. Combine the trip with shopping or sightseeing and the package is even more attractive.

Around 40 million Americans are either not insured medically or are underinsured. They cannot afford many procedures in the US but treatment for many in Asia is affordable even with the air fares. A procedure that might cost US$40,000 can cost as little as US$6,000 in Bangkok, for example, including the air fares and a private hospital room.

Europeans also are turning to Asia for treatment to avoid waiting times for operations and other procedures at home. And so US and European insurance companies and employers that provide medical benefits increasingly are covering air fares and medical expenses for hospitals in Asia.

A further fillip came after the September 11, 2001 terrorist attacks in the US. The US significantly tightened up on visas so that many foreigners, particularly from the Middle East, who might have sought medical treatment in the US, now find it too troublesome or impossible to get a visa, and instead travel to Asia for treatment.

Low-cost, high-quality medical care in Asia already attracts 1.6 million medical tourists. Most come from within the region but that is changing. The industry is growing 20–30% a year. One travel firm has estimated that Asia's medical tourism industry will generate US$4.4 billion a year by 2012, with Thailand, India, Singapore, and Malaysia being the leading medical travel destinations.[1] This is probably an underestimate.

Value for money is the main driver. Wage and salary costs are relatively lower in Asia. But a more important reason why Asia is price competitive is because the legal system in much of the region remains relatively poor. Simply, it's difficult to take legal action against a doctor or hospital for malpractice. And even if such action was possible and successful, the compensation is likely to be far less in most of Asia than in, say, the US. Accordingly, hospitals and surgeons do not need to carry the sort of legal indemnity insurance that is necessary in the US and elsewhere in the West.

Bumrungrad Hospital in Bangkok, a leading provider of services to medical tourists (see below) offers this in its promotional material:

> All patients in Thailand are protected by Thai law, codes of medical conduct, and a Patient Bill of Rights enforced by the Kingdom's Medical Council (you may ask the hospital for a copy). Patients may complain directly to the Thai Medical Council, or the Ministry of Public Health. These organizations have the power to enforce remedies because they grant licenses to hospitals and their doctors. You may also complain to the Thai Consumer Protection Agency or the police, or take legal action in a Thai court.

Essentially, this implies that your main recourse will be to attempt to have a doctor's license to practice revoked. You may take legal action too but only in a Thai court. But then, Thai courts are so notoriously inadequate and prone to corruption that even locals avoid using them.

If you are happy with there being little effective legal recourse, then medical procedures in Asia can be very cost-effective indeed: in short, the boom in medical tourism is another example of how, ironically, Asia profits from its poor rule of law.

Another risk is that the drugs used might be counterfeit. This is unlikely to be the case deliberately, but counterfeit pharmaceuticals are a big problem in all of Asia and can enter hospitals' supply chains inadvertently. This is a real risk in China, where some estimates are that around half of all pharmaceuticals sold are counterfeit. It is less of a risk in Singapore, where controls are more stringent.

Which countries are at the forefront of medical tourism in Asia? Thailand and India are shaping up to be the main beneficiaries. Singapore has long been a supplier of medical services to wealthy individuals in neighboring countries. It too will benefit but its cost structures are not nearly as competitive as, say, Thailand's. One reason for this is because Singapore has a more comprehensively functioning legal system: it's easier to sue a Singapore doctor. Malaysia too might benefit in future years. It has good local skills, or at least it would have if it could find a way to stop its best surgeons from emigrating, and a patchy legal system.

Thailand

Bangkok's Bumrungrad Hospital is perhaps the market leader in Asia when it comes to medical tourism. The 554-bed, for-profit hospital is listed on the Stock Exchange of Thailand. It has 19 operating theatres and claims to treat around 400,000 foreign patients a year. Many are holidaymakers in Thailand who unexpectedly need medical care. But increasingly, patients are foreigners who come specifically to Thailand for treatment at Bumrungrad – for example currently around 5,000 patients a month arrive for treatment from the Middle East. (To better cater to Middle Eastern clients, the hospital group is offering services in the Middle East itself – it signed an agreement in 2007 to operate a hospital in Abu Dhabi for example.) And when Bumrungrad was featured on the CBS News program *60 Minutes* in 2005, the hospital received thousands of enquiries from Americans seeking treatment the week after the program was aired.

The hospital even has a formal relationship with the worldwide travel company Flight Center so that patients can buy discounted air tickets to Bangkok and with Diethelm Travel so that once patients are in Thailand, they can book sightseeing tours. Interestingly, Bumrungrad does not employ foreign doctors; all of its almost 1,000 physicians are Thai.

Bumrungrad uses this as a selling point. Better an excellent Thai surgeon than a second-rate Western one.

Thailand's other main supplier of services to medical tourists is Bangkok Hospital, the flagship of Thailand's Dusit Medical Group. It claims to treat around 70,000 foreign patients a year.

But what sorts of procedure do these hospitals offer nonresident foreigners? The answer is pretty well anything. Cosmetic surgery is to be expected but more serious procedures such as hip replacements, hysterectomies, and kidney transplants are available.

Some Thai hospitals advertise in inflight magazines. Advertisements for Bangkok Hospital's branch at the Thai seaside resort city of Pattaya show images of a palm-fringed island surrounded by deep blue sea superimposed in an intravenous drip bottle. The 350-bed hospital offers a wide range of medical procedures. Patients are met at the airport by hospital representatives and offered special hospital corporate rates at nearby hotels. The hospital also provides translators for 22 different languages and can arrange tours to see the local sights.

India

India, like other Asian medical destinations, has capitalized on the post-September 11 paranoia of the US. Many wealthy Middle Eastern, African, and Asian patients, who would otherwise have traveled to the US for medical treatment, have found getting visas for the US troublesome, if they can get them at all. India, like Thailand, has been a beneficiary.

Currently, medical tourism is worth around US$350 million to India, with more than 150,000 foreigners seeking treatment in India annually. Many of India's existing health tourists come from Bangladesh, Pakistan, Malaysia, Japan, Singapore, the Middle East, and Africa. A McKinsey study commissioned by the Confederation of Indian Industry estimated in 2006 that the Indian healthcare industry was then worth more than US$20 billion annually but would grow to US$60 billion by 2012. It further estimated that India could earn more than US$2 billion from healthcare tourism by then.[2]

The Indian government then launched an aggressive campaign to market India as a destination for medical tourism, citing this potential US$2 billion in earnings by 2012. Its marketing campaign sought to portray India as a "holistic" health destination and showed women practicing yoga exercises on a beach and lying in baths replete with rose petals. The advertising suggested that treatment could also be combined with visits to the Taj Mahal or the Himalayas.[3]

A big beneficiary will be the Apollo Group, India's largest chain of private hospitals with 38 hospitals. It openly touts for medical tourists and claims to have served 14 million patients from 55 countries. Its website includes a section for "international patients," with advice on how to plan the trip to India and how to pay. The Group's hospitals even accept travelers' checks. The Group is also opening hospitals in the Middle East, Sri Lanka, Bangladesh, and Africa.

India is an attractive destination for healthcare because many outside India are familiar with Indian doctors who live and work in their own countries. The US has more than 50,000 doctors from India, for example. This helps to promote India as a destination with sufficient medical expertise.

As with Thailand, cost is a big factor. A bone marrow transplant that might cost US$200,000 in Western countries costs around US$20,000 in India, orthopedic surgery that costs US$20,000 might cost US$5,000 in India, and so on. And as with Thailand, the legal system is unbelievably slow and unpredictable.

But India will need to do a lot of work to overcome not just foreigners' perceptions of India as chaotic, overpopulated, and disease-ridden but also the reality. Arriving in India by air hardly inspires confidence in the medical treatment that might await. Most of India's airports are a disgrace even by developing country standards, and the roads that lead from them are an education, to put it mildly, jammed with traffic, filled with potholes, and winding through slums as many of them are. To overcome this, the Indian government has proposed a scheme of "hand-holding" on arrival for foreigners who travel to India for medical treatment. Apollo Group hospitals already offer an airport pickup service for its nonresident foreign clients. India is behind Thailand as a medical tourist destination but its worldwide reputation for IT services will help to lend it an air of technical sophistication that it otherwise would not have.

Singapore and Malaysia

Singapore too is seeking to cash in on medical tourism. However, medical care in Singapore is not cheap by Asian standards. It has long been a supplier of more advanced medical care to Malaysians and almost any medical care to wealthy Indonesians and expatriates resident in Indonesia. Other patients now come from Russia, Bangladesh, and the Middle East.

The Singapore government claims that almost 400,000 foreign patients traveled to Singapore for medical treatment in 2006. It aims to attract one million foreign patients by 2012.[4] In 2007, it released more land in Singapore to be used for the construction of private hospitals.

Certainly, the Singapore government feels that medical tourism will be a big growth area in Asia, quite apart from Singapore. Its holding company Temasek and a Dubai-based partner acquired a 6% stake in Bumrungrad Hospital in 2006.[5] Temasek also has a stake in India's Apollo Hospitals.

The key private hospital operators in Singapore are Parkway Holdings (which operates Gleneagles Hospitals) and the Raffles Medical Group, the latter claiming that foreign patients account for more than a third of all its patients. Its core markets are Indonesia and Malaysia. It has set up representative offices in Indonesia, Vietnam, Myanmar, Sri Lanka, and India to help attract customers.

Malaysia too has the potential to be a medical tourism destination. Its low cost, relatively good infrastructure, and English-language abilities should all help. Pantai Holdings is the biggest private hospital chain in Malaysia, a large part of which was acquired by Singapore private hospital group Parkway Holdings in 2006. But for now, Malaysia's biggest problem is the brain drain of its best medical practitioners and surgeons to Singapore, Australia, and elsewhere. Mostly, they're ethnically Chinese and find Malaysia less attractive than in the past and other places more welcoming and appreciative of their talents.

The overall experience of a good hospital in Asia is a huge contrast with most people's experience of a US or a UK hospital. Word of mouth will be important for building up medical tourism to Asia from the West. It is an industry that is currently taxiing along the runway and about to take off. The only cloud on the horizon is that the rule of law might improve across Asia to the point that Asia's surgeons will need huge medical malpractice indemnity insurance. But if Asia can avoid that, then the future will be healthy.

Suggestions for Business Strategists and Scenario Developers

▶ Several Asian centers are emerging as prominent international suppliers of high standard, competitively priced surgical procedures. These centers will receive a further boost with the continuing decline in the cost of air travel.

▶ Suddenly, shares in listed private hospitals in Asia are more attractive, as this new source of high-yield patients emerges.

▶ Western healthcare groups increasingly will find that when they seek to establish operations in the Middle East, South India, or China, they will face competition from hospital groups based in Singapore, Thailand, and India.

Notes

1   The figures come from Abacas Travel and are cited in *Business Times*, "Medical tourism to become multibillion dollar industry," April 7, 2006.
2   *Business Times*, "India fast becoming a medical destination," April 10, 2006.
3   *International Herald Tribune*, "India's healthy appeal," August 31, 2006.
4   *Business Times*, "S'pore expanding medical capacity to tap new markets," January 23, 2007.
5   *Business Times*, "Temasek buys 5.94% of listed Thai hospital," January 21, 2006.

Growing Corporate Ownership by Charities in Asia

▷ Massive corporate philanthropy is taking off in Asia. In years to come, many of Asia's biggest companies are likely to be controlled not by families or governments but by private charities.

▷ It will see the money available for social and other programs increase dramatically. It will help with corporate governance too.

Corporate Asia is populated by family-owned and managed companies, state-owned enterprises, and foreign-run companies. But a new corporate animal is about to enter the jungle: the high-flying charitable trust.

Asia has a long way to go to reach the corporate charitable foundations that the US and Europe now have, but the trend is clear, spearheaded perhaps by Hong Kong billionaire Li Ka Shing. Li's largesse is an inspiration to other wealthy entrepreneurs in Asia, particularly other ethnic Chinese businessmen.

Li founded the Li Ka Shing Foundation in 1980 and refers to it as his "third son" (he has two sons, Richard and Victor). It is a major donor to education and healthcare – Li is believed to have given away more than US$1 billion through the Foundation. Most of it has gone to causes in Hong Kong and China.

An immigrant from mainland China, Li had his start making and selling plastic flowers. As he became more successful, he moved increasingly into providing services, albeit with infrastructure development – specifically providing port services in Hong Kong, mainland China, India, and elsewhere, and more recently becoming a major worldwide force in telecommunications services. By moving beyond the old cultural stereotype, Li has transformed his group of companies into one of Asia's first homegrown genuine multinationals. He is admired around the world rather than merely in Hong Kong as an astute investor. Along the way, he has made himself the world's ninth richest individual, with an estimated fortune of US$23 billion.

Li was an early investor in the European telecommunications group Orange, before selling out to Germany's Mannesmann Group in 2001 for a profit of more than US$15 billion. In January 2007, Hutchison agreed to sell its 67% stake in the Indian mobile phone operator Hutchison Essar to Vodafone for a profit of around US$9 billion. Li was also quick to get into 3G and is now a big player in this technology in Europe and Asia.

Li said in 2006 that ultimately he intends to transfer at least a third of his wealth to his Foundation. Should he give the lion's share of his holdings to his Foundation, then it would mean that ports – Li controls 12% of the world's port facilities – and telecommunications interests around the world and many other assets would ultimately be controlled by charity.

There is precedent for this: India's Tata Group. The Mumbai-based Parsee Tata family heads up a series of charitable foundations that are the major shareholders in the Tata Group. This means that Group and family head Ratan Tata, one of India's most important businessmen, essentially manages the sprawling, multibillion dollar Tata empire on behalf of the family's charitable foundations.

The Economist said of Ratan Tata: "He does not seem to be motivated by money, and talks constantly about fairness and doing the right thing." The Group, it adds, has a reputation for refusing to pay bribes and for treating workers well.[1]

Today the Tata Group encompasses 96 main companies in seven business sectors, including steel making, truck assembly, power generation, hotels, financial services, publishing, chemicals, and telecommunications. It also controls TCS, India's largest IT outsourcing company.

The Group bought Tetley Tea worldwide in 2000 for US$421 million, the truck division of South Korea's Daewoo for US$102 million in 2004, and in 2007, Europe's Corus steel-making group for a massive US$11.3 billion.

Ratan serves on the board of India's central bank and is a member of the Prime Minister's Council on Trade and Industry. Among his other public and charitable roles are his membership of the board of trustees of the RAND Corporation and the Ford Foundation and he serves on the program board of the Bill & Melinda Gates Foundation's India AIDS initiative.

Among the Tata trusts and institutions supported by the Tata family are the Sir Dorabji Tata and Allied Trusts, the Tata Institute of Social Sciences, the Tata Memorial Center for Cancer Research and Treatment, Tata Agricultural and Rural Training Center for the Blind, the National Center for the Performing Arts (in Mumbai), Sir Dorabji Tata Trust Center for Research in Tropical Diseases, the Sir Ratan Tata Trust, Tata Council for Community Initiatives, and the JRD Tata Ecotechnology Center.

The Ayala Foundation is a leading corporate donor in the Philippines. It supports a wide range of good works aimed at improving the welfare of ordinary Filipinos. The Foundation also has a US-based arm that encourages Filipinos there to contribute to social development programs in the Philippines. The Foundation was established by the Ayala family.

The family's Ayala Group has interests in real estate, water supply, automobile distribution, banking, and food production. It has a reputation for being prudent and conservative. Jaime Augusto Zobel de Ayala II serves as chairman of the family holding company, the Ayala Corporation, the group's mobile telephone operator Globe Telecom, and the Bank of the Philippine Islands. He also serves as co-vice chairman of the Foundation.

The family's professionalism and concern for sound management practice is exemplary by Asian standards. The family does not have private business interests that run parallel with their listed companies and so it is free of the conflicts of interests that many Asian family-controlled conglomerates have between the listed and privately held components. All Ayala businesses are listed or belong to a parent company that is. Few family members are involved in the Group's management and then only if they have the requisite professional skills. Also, the Group has been raising its accounting and disclosure practices toward international standards, ahead of that mandated by the Philippines' Securities and Exchange Commission and the Philippine GAAP.

In Malaysia, the Malaysian entrepreneur Syed Mokhtar Al-Bukhary has established the Al-Bukhary Foundation. He has poured millions into the Foundation to build mosques, schools, and hospitals. The Foundation has also built, stocked, and runs the Islamic Art Museum in Kuala Lumpur, a world-class institution that puts Malaysia's National Museum to shame. It is responsible for acquiring many fabulous Islamic art works on the international art market and bringing them to Malaysia.

Al-Bukhary has built himself up from almost nothing to be one of Malaysia's richest men. He has developed port facilities and an airport in southern Malaysia, as well as amassing interests in property, hotels, power stations, rubber plantations, banking, retailing, and construction. His companies are not family run. He uses professional managers throughout.

In late 2006, his MMC Corporation together with a local partner won an extraordinary US$30 billion infrastructure deal in Saudi Arabia to develop a new industrial and commercial city. It's a huge undertaking for any company let alone a Malaysian one.

A strong Muslim but a modern one, he does not believe that women should cover their hair or their faces and feels that Muslims should return to what they once were known for: commerce and the arts.

It is possible that Syed Mokhtar Al-Bukhary will ultimately inject some or all of his corporate holdings into his Foundation. This would see some of Malaysia's biggest companies and important infrastructure developments controlled by charity.

There are examples of corporate largesse in Asia. The incidence is growing. The trend has positive implications and not just for charity itself. Once ownership of companies is transferred to charitable foundations, typically their management is transferred from the founding family to professional managers. Also, the interests of the charity tend not to cut across the interests of other shareholders and so corporate governance tends to improve as a result. The situation is analogous to the Crown Property Bureau (CPB) in Thailand, the private investment vehicle of the Thai royal family. The CPB owns controlling stakes in some of Thailand's most important and better run companies such as Siam Cement. Management is entirely professional – the royal family stays out of management altogether – and CPB companies are known for their compliance with the law and tax requirements.

Khoo Teck Puat, a Malaysian who lived in Singapore and owned almost 15% of Standard Chartered Bank at the time of his death in 2004, established the Khoo Foundation in 1981 to contribute mostly to medical, healthcare, and education causes. After his death, 30% of his fortune or US$1.5 billion was transferred to the Foundation. Another US$3 million went to Singapore's National Dialysis Foundation and several million more went to another Singapore institution to buy a major collection of Tang Dynasty ceramics.[2] In 2007, the Foundation and/or the family gave US$60 million to the National University of Singapore (NUS) to fund medical research, another US$13 million to establish a cancer research institute, and US$82 million to help build a 550-bed hospital.

Another important Singapore foundation is the Yong Loo Lin Trust, established by another business family. In 2005, the Trust gave US$70 million to the NUS School of Medicine and, in 2003, it gave US$20 million to the NUS for its Conservatory of Music.

In the Philippines, John Gokongwei, the founder of one of the country's biggest business groups JG Summit Holdings, announced in 2006 that he intended to fold 25% of his corporate holdings in JG Summit into a charitable foundation.[3] The foundation will help the country's poor and needy. Gokongwei is an admirer of the charity work of the Hong Kong billionaire Li Ka Shing and was inspired by him to make his gift. JG Summit Holdings is highly diversified, with operations in property, banking, finance, food, petrochemicals, textiles, hotels, power, cement, and telecommunications. A quarter of all that will now be put to work for charity.

When Hong Kong billionaire property investor Nina Wang died in 2007, two wills emerged. One, drawn up while Wang was stricken with cancer, appeared to leave her conglomerate Chinachem to her feng shui adviser. But an earlier will, drawn up in 2002 when Wang was healthy, outlined plans for an Asian version of the Nobel Prize and a range of other charitable works, the funds being administered by the UN secretary general, the Chinese government, and the chief executive of Hong Kong's administration.[4] Which would win out was unclear and will be settled by the courts. But again, the intention was clear – billions were to be transferred to charity.

In India, the situation is less clear. Other than the Tata family (see above) India's big entrepreneurs are reticent about what, if anything, they have transferred to charitable foundations. Azim Premji, the force behind IT services giant Infosys, is an exception. He established the Azim Premji Foundation, which focuses on promoting IT among Indian schools, particularly in rural areas.

Very Welcome

Perhaps the Wallenberg family of Sweden provides a model for Asia's billionaires. Most of the family's corporate wealth is tied up in a series of charitable foundations, which ultimately control more than a third of the value of the companies listed on the Swedish stock exchange. Among the interests are large or controlling stakes in some of Europe's biggest corporate names including Saab, Electrolux, Scania, ABB, AstraZeneca, Ericsson, Husqvarna, Stora Enso, and SAS. The foundations donate millions each year to science, research, and arts programs in Sweden. The family says that the ownership of most of its businesses by charitable foundations has helped with corporate governance: the family does not consider that they own the assets and so they are not inclined to consume or destroy the companies' value.[5]

The Wellcome Trust is another model. The Trust is second only to the Bill & Melinda Gates Foundation in terms of assets, with a portfolio worth almost £14 billion (US$28 billion). Set up in the UK in 1936 on the death of pharmaceutical entrepreneur Sir Henry Wellcome, the Trust acquired all the shares in Wellcome's pharmaceutical company, The Wellcome Foundation, with the earnings to be used to support medical research and research into the history of medicine. Today the Trust spends more than £500 million (US$1 billion) annually on biomedical research, including the sequencing of the human genome, stem cell research, and the development of antimalarial drugs.

The Trust is a ruthless corporate player, protecting its financial interests. It decided to diversify away from its single asset of the Wellcome Foundation and so, in 1986, floated the Foundation on the stock exchange. A quarter of its stake was sold off, and the proceeds were invested in more shares, property, and investment funds. More shares were sold in 1992 and the rest were sold off in 1995, when the company was bought by Glaxo to form GlaxoWellcome. (This entity later merged with SmithKlineBeecham in 2000 to form Europe's biggest pharmaceutical firm GlaxoSmithKline.)

The Trust is currently the UK's biggest investor in private equity and has around £6 billion (US$12 billion) invested in venture capital and hedge fund assets. And in 2006, it became the first charity outside the US to issue bonds, raising £550 million (US$1.1 billion). In addition to its own highly professional management, Wellcome employs more than 300 external fund managers.[6]

In 2007, the Trust was considering a takeover of Alliance Boots, one of the UK's largest pharmacy chains. In addition, the Trust has direct stakes in more than 20 smaller life science and healthcare companies.

In short, the Trust is extremely powerful. It allocates almost as much to medical research each year as the UK government's Medical Research Council but is completely independent of government. It will not be long before Asia has some Wellcome Trusts of its own.

Suggestions for Business Strategists and Scenario Developers

▶ There will be a greater demand for professional managers and for more corporate restructuring, as ownership of some of Asia's bigger companies is passed to charitable trusts.

▶ The removal of family ownership will also see such companies better and more prudently managed, with returns being the chief decision driver rather than, say, obscure factors relating to the interests of a controlling family.

▶ The link with professional management and the charitable element is also likely to see such companies pursue corporate social responsibility obligations more closely and steer away from the payment of bribes and other corrupt practices.

Notes

1   *The Economist*, "The shy architect," January 13, 2007.
2   *Business Times*, "Eric Khoo, charity get lion's share of Teck Puat's estate," September 14, 2006.
3   *Business Times*, "Gokongwei donates 25% of JG to the poor," August 16, 2006.
4   The *Guardian*, "Asia's richest woman leaves her fortune to feng shui master," April 21, 2007.
5   *The Economist*, "Sweden's enduring business dynasty," October 14, 2006.
6   The *Independent*, "Wellcome Trust in change of strategy with move on Boots," April 12, 2007.

Index